ROCKALL
SOLO

ROCKALL SOLO

45 days of Discipline, Optimism and Endurance

NICK HANCOCK

Copyright © Nick Hancock 2015

All photos and diagrams © Nick Hancock unless otherwise stated

Cover photo: Chris Murray QGM
Author photo: Michael Schofield

Nick Hancock has asserted his right to be identified as the author of this Work in accordance with the Copyright, Designs and Patents Act 1988

First published by Nick Hancock in 2015

www.nicholashancock.com

A CIP catalogue record for this book is available from the British Library

ISBN: 978-1500680886

For Freddie

CONTENTS

Illustrations & Diagrams		9
Forward		11
Preface		15
I	History	19
II	Rockall	23
III	2012	35
IV	The RockPod	52
V	2013	60
VI	Food and Water	67
VII	2014 Expedition Diary	70
Postscript		234
A	Entomology Report	237
B	Ordnance Survey Report	242
C	Bibliography	244
Acknowledgements		245

ILLUSTRATIONS & DIAGRAMS

Kerguelen's map of the Rockall area, Paris 1771	Page 21
Extract from 'The First Map of Rockall' RGS/IBG 1971	Page 25
Extract from notebook, showing Hall's Ledge and Southern elevation of Rockall	Page 27
Initial design drawings for the RockPod	Page 52
Extract from notebook showing light beacon measurements	Page 121
WindGuru Forecast for period 30th June to 4th July 2015	Page 166
Extract from notebook showing the baseline and transects for geomagnetism survey	Page 189

FOREWARD

Reproduced with permission, Ben Fogle

I am fixated by Rockall. It is a place that has captivated me since I was a child. A rock that has haunted me for many years. I made several unsuccessful attempts to land on Rockall myself. Rockall is a place that gets under your skin. Drawing you in. She is so close and yet so far. So small and yet so impenetrable. She teases you. On a calm day she looks calm and placid, in the more ubiquitous bad weather she looks terrifying. Like a fortified castle in the middle of the ocean. She has defeated many and satisfied few. Rich in history and legacy.

I fought Mother Nature and lost. The closest I ever got was to touch her damp walls. I was able to stick a post it note on her vertiginous wall laying claim to this controversial rock. And then along comes Nick Hancock who blows my attempt out of the water. A thrilling, brave, funny, eccentric attempt to settle one of the most intriguing 'islands' in the Atlantic.

Nick's expedition captivated not just the country, but the world. Indeed I was able to chat to Nick via Skype for NBC's Today show. In some ways that means my voice, if not my body, has made it onto Rockall. One day I will try again. Until then, she is Mr Hancock's, a very worthy custodian indeed. Bravo!

Ben Fogle, January 2015

RAF official photograph, 11 March 1943

PREFACE

It's not easy to say why, on a personal level, I wanted to undertake this challenge. There is the obvious benefit of raising money for Help for Heroes, but in some ways that is secondary to the challenge itself, because there are far easier and more conventional ways to raise money for charities, most of which I have already done: climb mountains, run marathons, etc. Again, with those challenges, it was the personal challenge first for me, then the thought that if I'm doing this somewhat selfish project, why don't I use it to benefit others too? None of that answers the question of why I wanted to do this or any of the other challenges I have completed before this one, and I suspect there is not a simple or satisfactory answer.

It had always been my intention at school to join the regular army, and to this end I passed my RCB (Regular Commissions Board) at 18 and was awarded an Army Bursary through university. I attended the OTC (Officer Training Corps) for four years while at university, and was privileged enough to be sent on attachment with them to the US Army on Fort Bragg, and through my sponsoring regiment, the now merged 1QLR (Queen's Lancashire Regiment) I travelled to Germany and Canada on attachment. These experiences pushed and challenged me more than any others during my life to that point, and what is more, I enjoyed them, learning a lot about myself on the way, and discovering that my capacity at that age to adapt and learn seemed limitless.

I don't mean that to sound arrogant; I suspect that we all have this capacity within us, it's just that we either choose not to push ourselves, preferring instead the safe regularity of normal life, or that we don't have the opportunity to, or have no one to show us that we can be, do and achieve more than the norm. I was lucky, I had the experiences, and I had my grandfather, Cliff, who since as far back as I can remember was the major influence in my life until he died in 1999. I have to admit that after his death I wandered for a few years, fairly none directional, quitting my job in London and heading off to see the world, working in China, India and Nepal as a guide and mentor to 'charity challengers' and students.

But life is about balance, and that was not enough for me. I also wanted a happy and stable family life, a secure income, and a home of my own. One has to make sacrifices, and having chased the dream of working in the outdoors and travelling successfully, I saw the benefits of the nine-to-five. Through some pretty dark times, I thought about, wrote down and planned how I'd like the next few years of my life to pan out. I couldn't get on with my plan of action immediately as I had agreed to work in India for two months, but I used that time to polish my CV, resurrect old business contacts, and make initial enquiries with recruiters with the plan of going back into property, and qualifying as a Chartered Surveyor, which I felt in a volatile market would at least give me some job security.

Having achieved that, getting a good job and buying my first flat, I was made redundant in early 2008 at the start of the recession. It had for a long time been a goal of mine to move to Scotland, I had friends and family up there, loved the mountains, and in 2007 had been up there no less than thirteen times from London for various reasons. Redundancy was the catalyst, I rented my flat out and moved North, with the added benefit of an instant girlfriend, as I'd met Pam the year before at a wedding in Edinburgh and we'd stayed in touch. However, there was no work. Everyone was cutting back and shedding staff, and I had no contacts nor experience in Edinburgh or anywhere else in Scotland. Ever the optimist, I took a job working in an outdoor clothing shop, so at least I could get cheap clothing and continue going out to the hills; then getting a job became my job.

It was bored one day at the cash register in the shop that I decided I needed another medium term goal, and thought that some sort of challenge would fit the bill and keep me occupied in the planning; it was early 2009. My first idea was to sea kayak from mainland Scotland to St. Kilda, forty miles out beyond the Outer Hebrides. I had experience of sea kayaking while working for John Ridgway in Sutherland at his adventure centre, before I went to China for the first time, and loved it. I had additionally always wanted to go to St. Kilda, and the Outer Hebrides, and this challenge offered the opportunity to do both. At this point I had not even heard of Rockall.

Sections of this trip had been completed before, but I wanted to combine them into one larger expedition, in the hope of achieving a 'first' and perhaps setting some sort of record, more for my own motivation than any other reason, as it was going to take a lot of training and I'm one of those people who can't just get or stay fit for the sake of it. I need a goal.

It was during the initial process of researching the route and outline logistics for this trip that I first heard of Rockall. In 1686 a ship was wrecked on or near the rock and the survivors, Spanish and French sailors, managed to limp to St. Kilda[1]. My research went the opposite geographical direction and soon I was enthralled in the history of Rockall, reading everything I could on the internet, obtaining a copy of James Fisher's[2] seminal book on the rock, along with James Macintosh's[3] pamphlet.

Before long I knew I wanted to visit Rockall, which at this point was generally accepted to have had less than one hundred people land on it[4]. Furthermore, having become aware of Tom McClean's solo occupation of forty days in 1985 and Greenpeace's group occupation in 1997 of forty two days, during the course of my research, I resolved to try and not just visit and land, but also to beat those existing records.

Somewhat naively I thought that two full years of organisation and preparation would be sufficient, and I christened the outline expedition 'Rockall 2011', thinking that I would be able to land around the two hundredth anniversary of the first recorded landing by Lieutenant Basil Hall RN[5] in 1811, after whom Hall's Ledge on Rockall is named.

---

[1] Martin Martin (1698)
[2] James Fisher (1956)
[3] James A. Macintosh (1946)
[4] Through my research, at the date of publication, I have identified at least 139 individuals who have landed, including myself, three of whom have landed at least twice.
[5] Basil Hall (1831)

Two years later, with insufficient funding, no boat, and only a partially constructed shelter I was forced to re-evaluate...

CHAPTER I

HISTORY

The story of Rockall is told by the history of the landings made on this remote rock, and also the failures to land and the attempts that never left shore. It's about the people, both men and women, who are drawn to this special place in the middle of the North Atlantic, whatever their varied and colourful reasons for going there.

The deep history of Rockall is shrouded in myth and legend. We have Basil Hall's own account of the 'discovery' and landing on Rockall in 1811, and with the turn of the twentieth century, landings were better recorded, with James Fisher's book including detailed research into the history of the rock. From this date onwards, many of the landing have been military, and so formally recorded, or by adventurers and yachtsmen whose photographs, film footage and reports have been widely reported and now recorded, in part, on the internet. My own research for this expedition inevitably turned up anecdotes, stories, contacts and records which I have begun to collate separately on the website of The Rockall Club[6], which I set up in 2012, along the lines of the St. Kilda Club[7].

Rockall is the remnant core of an extinct volcano, and is probably around fifty two million years old[8]. In terms of its human history, the earliest written record of the rock is traditionally thought by some to be from the seventh century in *Navigatio Sacti Brendani*, but St. Brendan 'The Navigator' left no written evidence or oral detail to say with any certainty that one of the many islands he landed on was indeed Rockall[9].

---

[6] www.therockallclub.org
[7] www.stkildaclub.com
[8] Geological Conservation Review, 1992
[9] Little (1946)

Following this, there is map evidence that Rockall was known to early sailors, although perhaps its position had not been confirmed. Fisher's research[10] indicates that the earliest map to show Rockall is in the British Museum, and dates from 1606, where the rock is identified as 'Rocol'. Throughout the 1600s, a number of maps and charts were produced which variably identified the island, and named it 'Rochol', 'Rokol', 'Rookol'. In 1703, Martin Martin's map in his *A description of the western isles of Scotland* showed 'Rokol' in the margin.

The earliest surviving written description is by Captain W. Coats in 1745, "Rokele is a pyramid not unlike [Sule] Stack, but higher and bigger, and white from the same cause."[11] Then in 1771, Rokol appeared on a French map[12] sixteen miles North of Rockall's known position in 1956, followed in 1809 by a description by Richard Peacock[13]: "This rock appears almost like a ship at distance".

Perhaps landings had been made by passing whalers, traders and fishermen before 1811, but this is the date of the first recorded landing[14] on Rockall, by a party from HMS Endymion, which included Lieutenant Basil Hall and others. It was Hall[15] who described Rockall as, "This mere speck on the surface of the waters... The smallest point of a pencil could scarcely give it a place on any map, which should not exaggerate its proportions...". The feature now known as Hall's Ledge was named by James Fisher and his party in 1955 after the only man in this first landing party whose name they knew for certain.[16]

Through the remainder of the nineteenth century, there were a number of recorded landings and unsuccessful expeditions to Rockall, which I will not go into here, save to remember the loss of 'The Helen' in 1824, which gave the

---

[10] James Fisher (1956), page 16
[11] in John Barrow, *ed.* (1852)
[12] De Kerguelen(1771)
[13] in Purdy (1812)
[14] James Fisher (1956) p.23
[15] Basil Hall (1831)
[16] James Fisher (1955) p.35

name to Helen's Reef to the East of Rockall, and the wreck of 'The Norge' on the same reef in 1904, with at least six hundred and thirty lives lost.

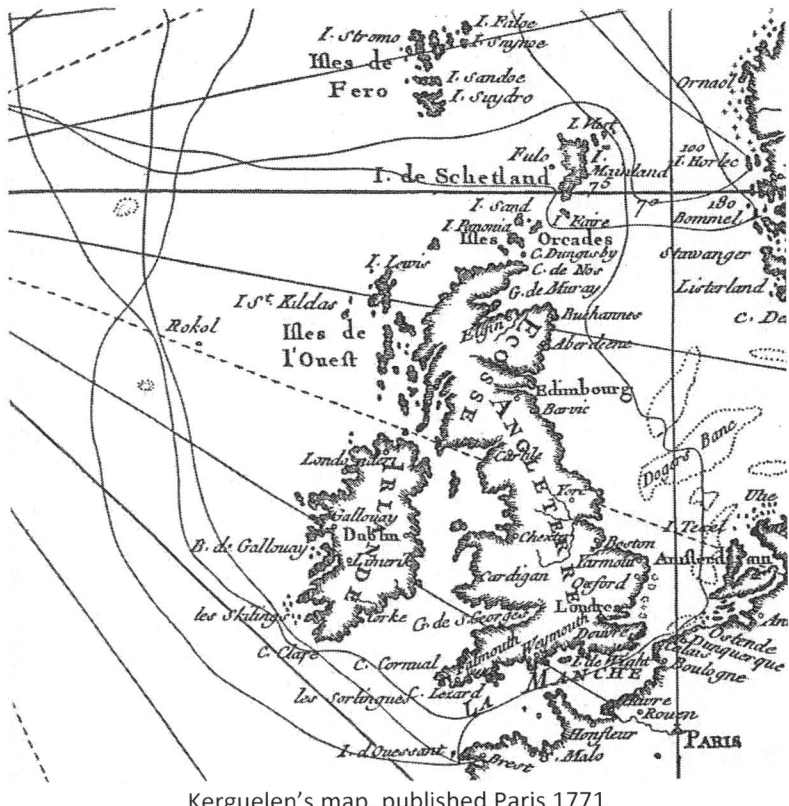

Kerguelen's map, published Paris 1771

In the book about his landing, Fisher coined the phrase, "the smallest isolated rock, or the most isolated small rock, in the oceans of the world". Fisher was a naturalist, who accompanied a team from HMS Vidal in the official annexation of Rockall in 1955 on behalf of Her Majesty The Queen. More landings followed, but the next significant event was the removal of the summit peak of the rock in 1971 by 39 Regiment Royal Engineers, in order to facilitate the installation of a navigation light in 1972. The flat area at the summit, that this operation left, was a boon for me in that it was an additional 'safe' flat area where I could stand and sit outside my pod.

Again, there were further landings after this date, which I don't intend to go into as they are not wholly relevant to my story, but if you are interested in knowing more about them, I would point you towards The Rockall Club.

Then, in 1985, Tom McClean an ex-Parachute Regiment and former SAS soldier, and veteran of various solo Atlantic challenges, landed by boat on Rockall with the assistance of the Royal Navy. The purpose of his occupation was to re-affirm Britain's mineral and oil rights in the area[17]. Tom spent forty days on Rockall, from 26th May until 4th July, living in a home-made plywood box, sponsored by Milbury Homes, tethered to the rock with pitons and nylon ropes, thereby inadvertently setting the solo occupation record that I hoped to surpass. I met briefly with Tom in the very early stages of my planning, in Liverpool after a talk he gave in 2010, and from my short chat with him gleaned some useful insights into living on Rockall and for my shelter design.

Yet again, additional landings followed, but the next one of serious interest to me was by Greenpeace in 1997. On the 10th of June they landed by helicopter and subsequently declared a new global state which they declared the Republic of Waveland[18]. The Greenpeace team was rotated from their support vessel, MV Greenpeace, and lived in a Kevlar reinforced survival pod, designed by Al Baker, one of the team, for a total of forty two days, setting a new group and longest occupation record. I have corresponded with Al on numerous occasions throughout my preparations for Rockall Solo, and he has been an extremely helpful guide and advisor.

---

[17] www.motivationspeaker.co.uk/Biography.asp
[18] www.waveland.org/history.html

CHAPTER II

ROCKALL

When Miller Christy said in 1898 that "To the average person, the existence of the locality known as Rockall is almost, or wholly, unknown. It might form part of the British Isles, or be situated in Central Asia, so far as the ordinary man is able to tell", he could well have been writing today.

To some the sea area in the North Atlantic is know from the BBC's Shipping Forecasts, but few would know that the area is named after the small rock that exists out there, some 248 miles West of Leverburgh on the Isle of Harris in the Outer Hebrides and around 187 miles further out to sea than St. Kilda, which is viewed by many as the western edge of the British Isles. In fact, Rockall is so far off shore, it's in a different time zone to the rest of the United Kingdom, being UTC -1, the same as Eastern Greenland and much of West Africa. The boat I chartered to take me to Rockall took fifteen hours each way to cover this distance, at an average speed of sixteen knots.

Rockall is comprised of a course grained granite. It consists primarily of quartz, feldspar and mica, with a few minor minerals such as aegirine and riebeckite. The term 'Rockallite', which was originally used for the stone from the island, is now no longer in use. Rockall is composed of moderately coarse-grained granite with small areas of finer grained micro-granite. The granite contains cavities which contain a variety of rare minerals, with sharp boundaries between the inclusions and the granite, and was probably formed as a small intrusion at a late stage in Tertiary igneous activity. [19]

The summit of Rockall is tear drop in shape and almost flat, due to the fact that the Royal Engineers blew the previously pointed summit peak off in 1971 during 'Operation Tophat'. The reason for this was to place a navigation light on the top of Rockall to aid shipping in the area. Their method was to drill parallel lines through the summit cone and place explosives in the

---

[19] Geological Conservation Review, 1992

resulting voids. The eleven drill tracks are still plainly visible, each being about four centimetres wide, and formed the basis for the grid I used to measure and subsequently draw the summit plateau and its features. Between the individual drill tracks the rock is not perfectly flat, but in some areas it has been levelled properly in order to place several plaques.

There is now just one plaque on the summit, commemorating the 1971 light beacon, which is generally central to the summit plateau. My feeling is that this may have been moved from a previous location on the summit further to the West as there is a similarly shaped flat area there, with four corresponding bolt holes but no plaque. It is on this flat area, where a plaque may previously have been, that I placed my survey marker for the GNSS survey I carried. This was due to its level nature and before the storm scoured the summit revealing the bolt holes. Had I known that there had historically been a plaque in this location I would have positioned the survey marker differently.

The main feature on the summit is the cone of the light beacon housing which Greenpeace repaired in 1998, replacing the original light as it had been damaged almost immediately after it was installed. The housing is red in colour, round and about five metres in circumference and appears to be made from fibre glass, being two centimetres thick in places, with a white line on the exterior facing approximately North. On my arrival at Rockall there were a number of Guillemots using the housing for shelter; this is by far the smelliest place on the rock, not aided by there also being several broken and abandoned eggs in amongst the guano and dead birds. I think it unlikely that the eggs laid in the housing ever hatch, as there was water up to the ledge inside the housing that the birds were resting on, which drained in the run up to a large storm that I experienced, but afterward had refilled to above the ledge level.

(There follows a comprehensive description of the natural and man-made features of Rockall, which I have included as a continuation of James Fisher's record of the rock, but which the less historically minded reader may wish to skip – I won't be offended!)

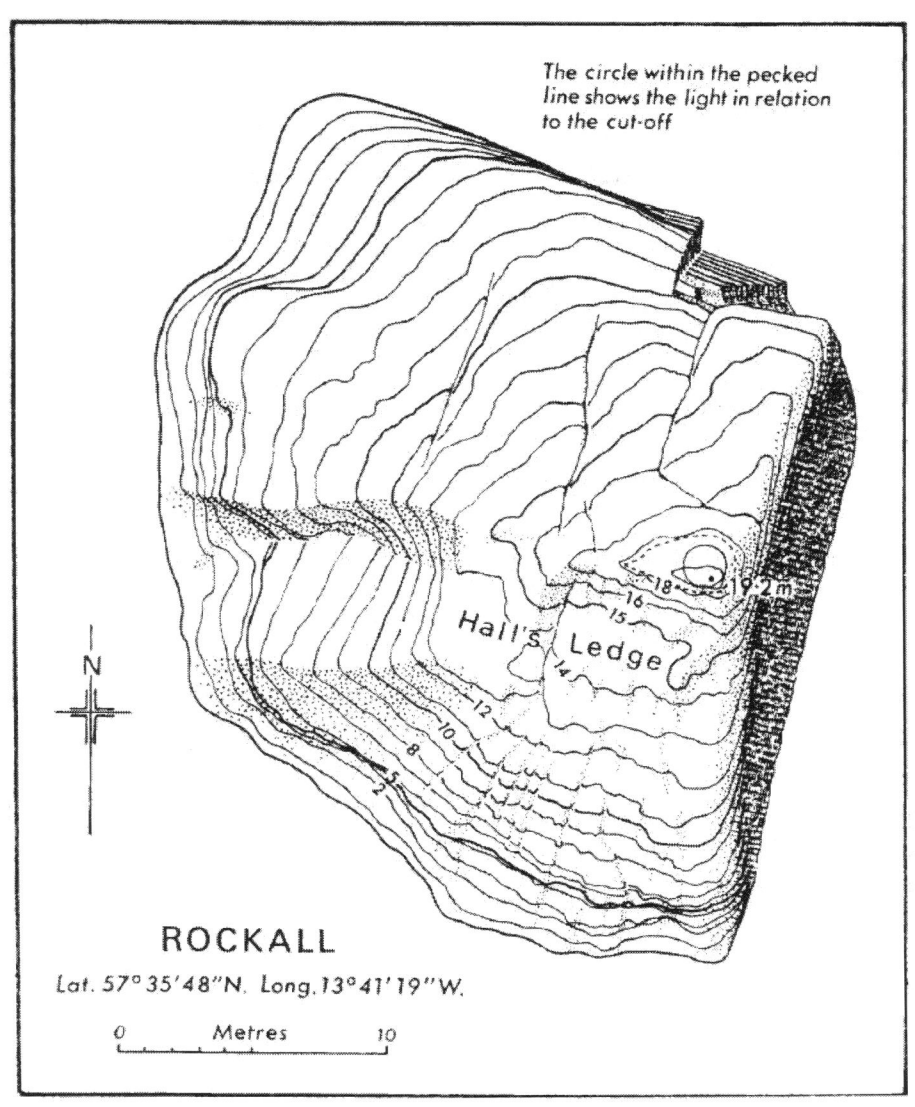

© Royal Geographical Society (with IBG)

Beyond the housing at the East end of the summit are two Raumer-type hanging plates, one of which I placed to tether a guy wire for my wind turbine. On the South side of the housing are four bolts, forming a square, which from photographs I have studied appear to be from the wind turbine base that Greenpeace used during their stay on the rock. To the West of the housing, between it and the plaque was the location of the base of my wind turbine. To the north of this is an individual Petzl Collinox-type fixing left over from Greenpeace's occupation. To the South of the plaque, on the edge of the summit is a second fixing, with a third, also on the Southern edge, approximately 1.2 metres further west. These three fixings form a triangle, who's other two sides measure roughly 1.2 metres by 1.8 metres.

The other main feature on Rockall is 'Hall's Ledge', which has historically described the whole of the roughly flat area that sits about three metres below the summit on the Southern flank of the rock. Over the course of my stay, I came to split the Ledge into named sections, as it is not a contiguous flat ledge, but is actually made up of several distinct features, all of which are formed from separate flows of lava or subsequent cracking. Unlike on the orientation shown in 'The First Map of Rockall', which was drawn from aerial photographs, my measurements indicate that the ledge runs almost exactly East to West, and so faces almost due South, which means that the true orientation of Rockall may need to be adjusted slightly on that map (below).

At the East end of the ledge there is a small area about a metre wide and around two and a half metres long which runs along the top of the obvious East facing cliff of Rockall. This area, which I christened the 'The East Step', slopes from North to South at a low angle and is characterised by rough, relatively sharp rock features, and a jumble of steps and ledges towards the edge of the cliff. There are two rusting old rock pitons in this area, as well as two larger rock core sample holes (Type 1) which are about five centimetres in diameter.

Moving west, there is a step up from the East Step onto Hall's Ledge proper, which is near vertical at the Southern end progressing to a slope at about sixty to seventy degrees at the northern end where it meets the wall at the back of Hall's Ledge. The main ledge is actually split into two distinct, roughly triangular areas by a large crack which is curved and runs diagonally across the ledge from north-east to south west, forming a shallow gully between the two sections in the flatter area. Part of this gully, at the southern end, has been filled with concrete and there is the remnants of a sawn off metal leg sticking out, which I believe is part of the tripod used to erect the Union Jack when Rockall was annexed in 1955.

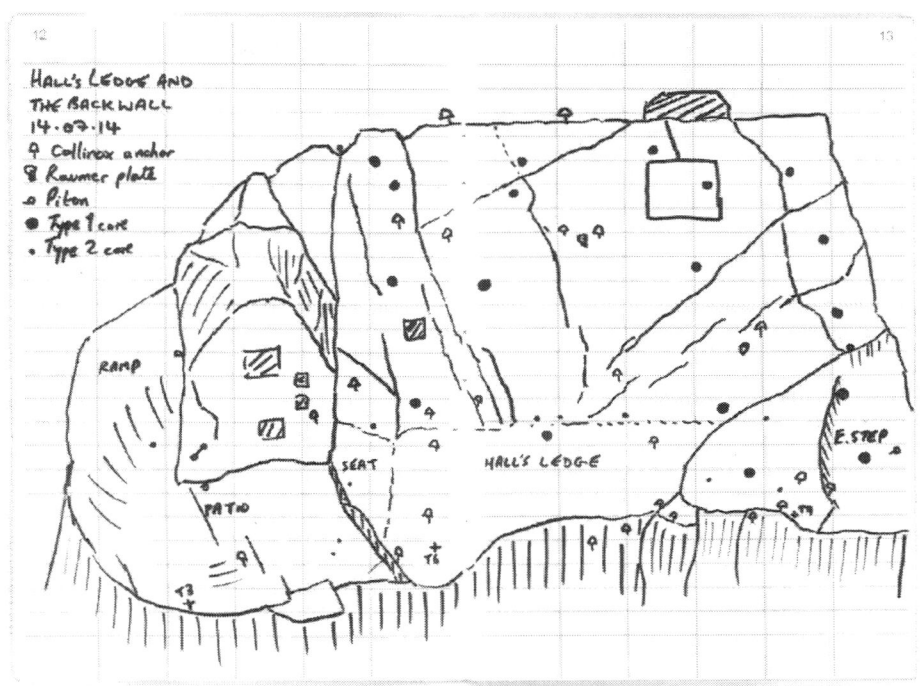

Extract from note book, drawn from RockPod 14th July 2014

The easternmost triangular section (Section One) is vaguely domed with some small rock features. It is a little over two metres wide at the southern edge, and approximately two and half metres deep along the East Step. There are three small, old and rusting ring bolts across the top of the domed area, running roughly north to south, which I think may have been placed by Tom McClean in 1985. In addition there are four stainless steel Collinox anchors in this area, placed by Greenpeace in 1997: two along the southern edge, one at the east edge on the threshold of the East Step, and a fourth roughly central and set a third of the way back in from the southern edge. Also in this area are four rock sample holes; one is fairly central (Type 1), the other three form a rough triangle and are smaller (Type 2) being about three centimetres in diameter; there is a fourth smaller hole, similar to Type 2 in this area which appears to be tentative and not completed. Finally, there is a rusting bolt in the crack at the bottom of the gully between Sections One and Two of Hall's Ledge.

The second part of the ledge (Section Two) is also roughly triangular, with the base of the triangle running along the back wall and the apex pointing out to sea. In fact this area is not broken from the back wall and forms part of the same piece of rock as the majority of the wall, tapering as a whole from the east edge of the summit and part way up the west end of the summit ridge, down to the point towards the sea. There is a definite transition in angle from the wall to the ledge in this area, but the transition is curved rather than abrupt. It was in this area that the original plaque was cemented to commemorate the annexation of Rockall in 1955, which went missing shortly afterwards, and it is also in this area that the RockPod was located, which unfortunately obscured most of the central area while I was in occupation. Looking beneath the pod, where possible, this part of the ledge appears to be gently undulating, with few central features save for a depressed area that collects water. At its widest, along the back wall, it is approximately three and a half metres wide, tapering to an apex in the south at which point the ledge is also around three and a half metres deep; although the final one and a half metres to the south slope down at a shallow angle.

There are eight Collinox anchors in this area, four of which form a rectangle around the position of the RockPod (one being within the gully described above, beside the concrete) and which were placed by me. The remaining four are split, with three being just beyond the southern edge of the ledge on the south face and on a prominent feature at the end of the gully which has been partially drilled and removed for rock samples, and the fourth being out on the west side of the sloping tip of the triangle, on the edge of the 'Western Step', which were placed by Greenpeace. Where visible, there are a number of rock core holes along the transition point with the back wall, of both types, a rusting bolt within the same main partition crack as the one above, and the remnants of one of Tom McClean's ring bolts where the ledge begins to slope towards the sea. For reference, point 'T6', where my transect number six meets the ninety degree baseline, as used in my geomagnetic and Hall's Ledge surveys, lies thirty eight centimetres West, along the baseline, of the Collinox anchor, which is also on the baseline, at the transition point of Hall's Ledge to the Western Step. I marked this point (T6) with a cross (+) and the numerals 'VI', so that it might be used to set up the baseline and transects again in the future.

The western edge of the main ledge is defined by what I called 'The Western Step' and 'The Seat'. The Seat is a ten centimetre deep depressed feature in the edge of the ledge, above the step, and adjacent to 'The Plaque Wall'. It holds some water, and is so named because it forms a comfortable seat, which would allow two people to sit cosily together facing West. Their legs would drop down the Western Step, which at this point is forty eight centimetres high, with their feet on 'The Patio', adjacent to The Plaque Wall. At its widest, the seat is approximately 1.1 metres wide by 0.75 metres deep. Around The Seat are three more of Tom McClean's ring bolts, and just above it on the back wall is Tom's partial carving of his name, 'Tom McCl', in the rock.

Beyond the western step is a wide flattish area, which I came to call 'The Patio'. There is no physical delineation between the patio and 'The Ramp' above, but for the purposes of this description I have drawn an imaginary line across the face of the plaque wall to the edge of the western face of Rockall. The cliff edge of the patio curves round from west to south facing, and as it does so the slope increases from being fairly level at the top to around thirty degrees in the middle section. There are few features save for a few minor bumps and grooves, until you reach the junction with the western step, where there is a narrow channel running along the junction. The patio and ramp appear to be one piece of rock, and separate in form from both Hall's Ledge (including the back wall), and the Plaque Wall and its associated ridge, with a crack running along the almost right angled junction between the Patio/Ramp and the Plaque Wall/Ridge. In this crack are two rusting old pitons, one at the foot of the Plaque Wall and one along the side of the plaque ridge, a little over half way up The Ramp.

There are few core holes in this area, with just one of Type 2 on the ramp and two of Type 2 on the patio. In addition, there is a single Tom McClean type ring bolt in the patio. The Ramp itself is really just a continuation of the patio, sloping approximately North-South with an angle varying from almost zero where it meets the patio, increasing to near forty five degrees at the top, where it meets the summit ridge and tips sharply over onto the northern face of the rock. At its widest, the ramp is about 2.3 metres wide and is approximately 4.3 metres long (depending on where exactly you place the transition to the patio). The patio is similarly circa 3.8 metres at its widest and about four metres at its deepest.

The back wall, above Hall's Ledge and the patio is split into two distinct areas by an obvious horizontal crack around quarter of the way in from the Western end. This crack runs over the summit ridge, before turning west down it and joining the top of the patio, where it runs as the defining line between the ramp and patio, and the Plaque Wall and ridge, forming a distinct block of separate rock. I named it 'The Plaque Wall' as there were two plaques on this almost vertical wall, which tapers to the top. This was the only grouping of plaques on Rockall when I arrived, and I added to it with a replica of HMS Tiger's plaque and the one for my Jubilee Expedition, so that there are now four. This seemed to me the best place to concentrate any plaques, rather than them being scattered haphazardly all over the rock, as it is a defined vertical wall of limited width. It is also my view that this would also be the ideal place for any replica of the original annexation plaque to be placed, replacing the duplicate Light Beacon plaque in the top centre of the wall.

Above the Plaque Wall itself, the block runs in a low ridge up to an almost right angled junction with the summit ridge, where there is a small vertical triangular section, which could also take a plaque if needed. Along the defining crack at the west side of the block, at The Ramp, the block is slightly undercut, and there is an old piton within the crack itself. There is a second piton in the crack at the base of the Plaque Wall, a Collinox anchor in the lower half of the wall itself, and an older long ring bolt in the lower eastern section which is probably only strong enough for temporarily securing kit, not people. The rock here appears to be slightly porous in nature, and when I cut the recesses for the plaques I noted that it seemed to be holding quite a bit of moisture. There is an area of moss growth on the eastern side of the small ridge, which may be evidence of this.

Moving east from the Plaque Wall, you come to the main section of the back wall which, as described above, also forms the main central section of Hall's Ledge below. The transition from ledge to wall is not defined, with a varying curved progression ranging from about twenty seven degrees to about fifty four degrees. There are three major cracks in this large section of wall, splitting it roughly into thirds. The first, western one runs down diagonally from left to right from the summit ridge to the ledge, where just before the ledge it splits into three distinct smaller cracks. The section of the wall to the west of this crack is thus roughly triangular in shape, tapering to the top. Within this block there are four larger core holes of Type 1 and one of Type 2 near the transition to the ledge; four Collinox anchors, one just over half way up and three more about quarter of the way up from the ledge in a line, one being positioned within the right hand of the three lower cracks. There is also a plaque dedicated to Tom McClean; an old threaded bolt just above the left hand most of the lower anchors; and a number of minor but distinct cracks.

The central section of the back wall trio is defined on its right hand edge by a crack from the summit to almost the ledge, running mostly parallel to the crack to its west (above). Within the top quarter of the wall, however, the crack changes angle, first to the left and then back more sharply to the right as it rises, with a 'tail' crack running back from the junction with the main crack, downwards towards the left. Above and below the top section of this crack are two Type 1 core holes, and a rusting ring bolt above. There is a further Type 1 core hole centrally, with a Type 2 at the foot of the wall where it becomes the ledge. There is one Collinox anchor in the upper half of this section, being roughly in line (slightly below) with the top anchor in the previous section.

The final, right hand (easternmost) section of the back wall is the largest of the three. The extreme right hand (eastern) edge of the section forms the top of the large east facing cliff of Rockall. The transition from back wall to east cliff is defined by an almost rippled section of rock running from the top to the bottom of the wall, where it becomes the east step. There are three Type 1 core holes in this section alone. Just over half way up this part of the wall is a deeper crack which runs diagonally down from right to left; it becomes less defined as it reaches further west and down, and is followed by a series of short parallel cracks beneath it, in its second half. The base of this section is clearly defined in part by the crack running through and splitting the main part of Hall's Ledge in two; the remaining part progresses smoothly into Hall's Ledge, as with the preceding sections. Within this crack, towards the eastern end, are two rusting pitons, which appear to have been concreted in.

There are three Type 1 core holes in this section, along with four Collinox anchors: two just over half way up and in line; one half way between these and the base, towards the east; and another towards the bottom, beside the crack that separates this block from the one to its west. The largest man-made feature on this section is the square metal frame of the solar panel housing associated with Greenpeace's replacement light beacon on the summit, which lies in the top half of the wall. The panel itself has gone, but the frame is intact, although slightly bent, with most of its bolts in place. There is a groove cut in the top of the frame which aligns with a groove cut into the rock above the frame and running up to the summit, where it meets one of the drill tracks containing a redundant wire and capped with a metal plate. It is therefore assumed that this grove was cut to house a wire powering the light beacon from the missing solar panel. There are also two Raumer-type hanging plates in this section of the wall: one I placed for a guy line for my wind turbine, which is between the upper two Collinox anchors, and an older one in the bottom right hand section of the rock. At the base of this section, where it becomes the ledge, are a single Type 1 and a single Type 2 core hole.

CHAPTER III

2012

I had originally intended to land on Rockall in 2011 to start my occupation, but was thwarted by lack of funds, the complexity of the logistics required to get there, onto and secured on Hall's Ledge, and the process of building my own shelter. I continued to work towards my goal throughout 2011, and became aware towards the end of the year that Kilda Cruises were due to launch a new boat in early 2012. This boat seemed ideal for my purpose, and would have the required offshore capability and license. Angus Campbell, the owner, wanted to go to Rockall in the new vessel, to be named Orca 3, to prove its capabilities for potential future commercial charters.

I met with Angus while on holiday on the Isle of Harris in June 2011 and we discussed my outline plans and his new boat, which was then under construction in Ireland. I had, in the meantime, also been corresponding with Angus Smith since August 2009, who had skippered his yacht, The Elinca, to Rockall and further afield on a number of occasions, and who, unbeknown to me at the time, would become the skipper of Orca 3 for all my future expeditions to Rockall. With the setbacks of 2011 behind me, I had hoped to be in a position to go to Rockall on the full expedition in 2012, but yet again it was not to be. The recession had not yet retreated and as hard as I tried, there was no funding to be had.

Instead, and having confirmed a charter with Angus Campbell during the winter of 2011 for the summer of 2012, with his consent I decided to go for a reconnaissance mission using the meagre funds I had; Angus would then be able to test his new boat and was additionally able to interest a number of other individuals in the prospect of landing on Rockall, albeit for probably only a few hours, in order to cover some of his costs.

As I had only limited personal kit and myself to take to Rockall in 2012, I drove up in my car from Edinburgh, via Callendar, Glen Coe and the Isle of

Skye. I camped overnight at Uig before catching the ferry over in the morning to Tarbert on Harris, where I was met by an employee of the Abhainn Dearg distillery, a former soldier, in order to collect the empty barrel I had organised to take onto Rockall. The plan as that this barrel would be filled on my return, the whisky finished and then auctioned off for Help for Heroes.

My next stop was the Blackhouse campsite at Lickisto, where we had stayed the previous summer, and where I had decided to base myself for this trip. Once camp was set up, I headed to Leverburgh to meet the rest of the team which included Pennie Latin from the BBC, who was going to film the landing attempt and make a piece for radio at the same time. The Scottish Sun sent Nick Sharpe and Michael Schofield to cover the trip; I had met both of them previously during the planning phase and when they photographed the winch practice sessions at Ratho. All of them, along with Bob Kerr with whom I had traded emails prior to the trip and Torquil Crichton, were staying at the Am Bothan bunkhouse in Leverburgh, run by Ruari Beaton who was to be a crew member alongside Pete Macdonald, who I first met on board the Orca 3.

The organisation for this trip was fairly informal, liaising with the skipper, Angus, by mobile phone and email for forecasts and likely departure dates. I didn't want anyone thinking this was my expedition; as far as I was concerned we were all paying our way and we should all have an equal chance of landing on the rock, but there was a definite air that this was primarily my reconnaissance.

At midday on Thursday 31st May we were loaded and ready to depart. Unfortunately, in the midst of loading and refuelling, while carrying out engine checks, Angus discovered that there was an oil leak into the engine cooling water. There followed some frantic calls to the boat builder, who confirmed that they had experienced this issue before and knew which part needed to be replaced. However, the part was in Glasgow, the engineer in Inverness, and the boat on Harris! Angus Campbell, the Orca 3's owner, decided that we couldn't head out in that state and that he would take the boat on one engine to meet the engineer and the couriered spare part in Uig on Skye. While the rest of us rested and slept, and Angus Smith helped Ruari finish off the new bathroom in his house, he headed off.

In the end, we had fourteen hours to kill. The group decided to head up to the North Harris eagle observatory. It was a pleasant, if wet thirty minute walk into the hut, for which we were not rewarded with the sight of an eagle, but there were some fairly peculiar characters in the hide which entertained us all, and gave us a topic to chat about and bond over. In the afternoon, we got word that we would probably be able to head out to Rockall that evening, and that we should meet the boat at Leverburgh pier when it returned from Skye in order to load up while they refuelled. It looked good, with a forecast clear window on site and reasonable swell for a few hours, which would mean that anyone who wanted to land should be able to.

Fortunately, the bunkhouse wasn't full, and we all took up residence in a small room above the living area, so that when Angus was back in range, he could call me, I would wake the others, and we could all rendezvous back at the pier and head out to the rock. I slept well, and the call came from Angus at about one in the morning on the 1st of June. An hour and a half later we were all up, ready, and down at the jetty, most of the equipment was already back on board, and the boat refuelled for the journey out into the Atlantic. I quickly texted home to say that we were on our way and updated Twitter before I finally lost signal on my mobile. From this point on we would have to rely on Bob's satellite phone which he had kindly agreed to let me use for the duration of this trip.

Orca 3 is equipped with eight bunks in the forward section, and I quickly got my head down for what promised to be a long cruise out. The throb of the engine and rhythm of the boat breaking the waves rapidly rocked me to sleep and I awoke after we passed St. Kilda, but just in time to see the archipelago disappearing behind us, which was a strange experience as it was planning to go there that had spawned this whole expedition in the first place. Having taken a few photos, I decided to get some more rest ahead of the coming challenge, particularly as there's not a lot to look at after St. Kilda. I slept through until we were well out, off the edge of the continental shelf and the sun had risen.

The rest of the journey out was spent chatting and getting to know 'The Angii', as I had only met Angus Campbell once before this trip, in a pub on Harris to discuss the expedition, and had never met Angus Smith in person, although we had communicated by email several times. They were both typical island and sea-faring men, of few words at that stage, obviously unsure of me, my motivations and ability, and I was acutely aware that these were the men I would be asking to risk their boat, equipment and crew in pursuit of my dream at some point in the future. I had to prove myself to them, they wouldn't suffer a fool (they'd seen one out here before) but equally I had to be sure I liked, trusted and got on with them too. I also had some interviews to do for the BBC with Pennie, along with the ubiquitous posing for shots for The Sun, chatting informally with Nick in order that he could send back a report once we returned to shore, and spotting sea birds and dolphins.

At around 1300 we were thirty eight nautical miles out from Rockall, cruising at sixteen knots on a heading of 266 degrees. We had passed the Anton Dohrn seamount, but were still in deep water, having not yet reached the edge of the Rockall Bank. Despite this, apprehension was building as we readied equipment and chatted about how we were going to tackle the attempted landing.

Unfortunately, by this time Torquil was extremely sea sick and Michael was not far behind him. I had prepared for the worst and was using both motion sickness wrist bands and anti-sickness pills prophylactically, in addition to having been watching what I'd been eating and drinking in the forty eight hours up to departure in the hope that I would avoid sea sickness; which I did. The sea state in deep water is different to inshore or over banks, and so we hoped that both Michael and Torquil might recover as we approached the rock, but this was not to be. For Torquil it meant that his hope of landing on Rockall was over, and he still had to endure the journey home; for

Michael, who had a job to do, it meant that he had to shoot photographs while holding back nausea; he didn't get as many photos as he'd hoped for!

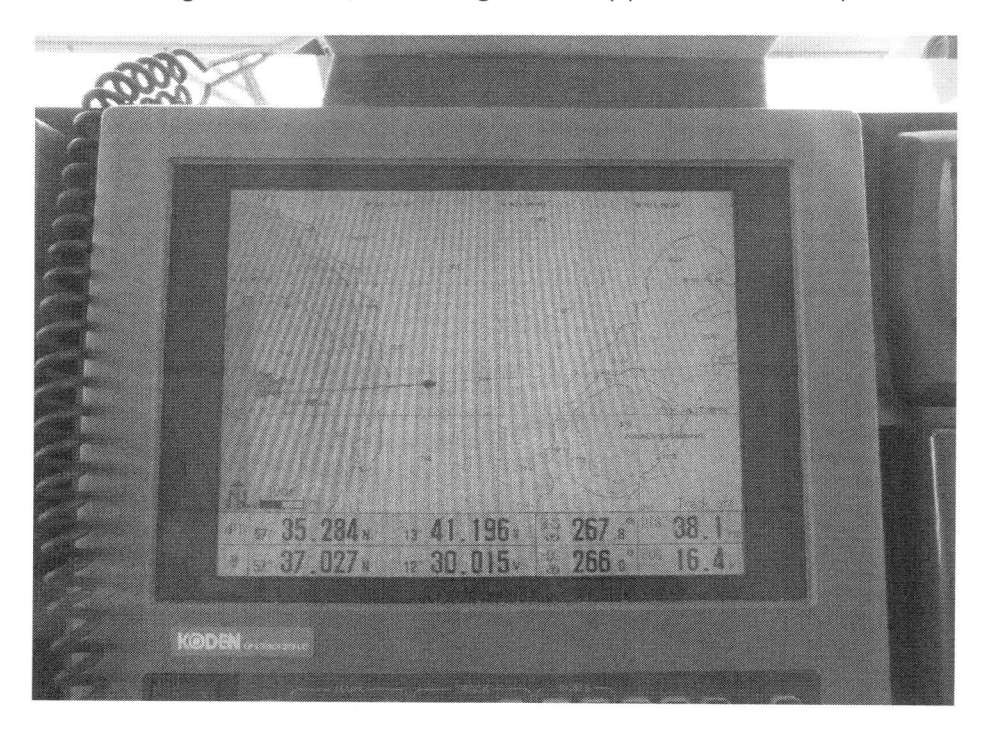

We finally sighted Rockall at about 1430 from seven miles out, after a twelve hour cruise. It still look another half an hour to draw close. As we approached the rock in the middle of the afternoon, it was for all of us, with the exception of Angus Smith, our first ever sight of it. We knew, because of the delayed departure, we had less time on site than we had hoped for due to forecast degrading weather, and it was obvious that the sea state was not ideal, with waves breaking all around the base of the rock. We made a lap of the Rockall in Orca 3 in order to spot the landing point and assess the conditions in more detail. Angus asked me if I wanted to go for it, which having come that far I did, and he agreed that we should make an attempt. Donning my kit, I remember feeling excited more than anything. I wore light weight but warm walking gear under a Safequip dry suit and buoyancy aid, second hand Vibram soled dry suit boots from eBay, a plastic climbing helmet from the BBC with a GoPro camera attached, neoprene gloves to protect my hands on the rocks and keep them warm, and a light weight rope tied securely around my back in a backpack-style, so that I had something with which to pull up some test bags of equipment once I was on Hall's Ledge.

Bob, similarly attired, climbed into the rigid inflatable boat (RIB) alongside me, once it had been lowered into the water around one hundred metres off the rock, along with Pete who as a scallop diver was the strongest swimmer and would be our safety man, and Angus Campbell who would helm the tender. Michael had no intention of leaving Orca 3. I don't think Torquil was capable of leaving even if he'd wanted to, and Angus Smith remained on board as skipper. Pennie had been ordered not to leave the boat and attempt to land by the BBC, and Nick had decided he would have a go if time and conditions allowed. We had at some point decided that I would have the first attempt at landing, and once we had approached what my research suggested was the best landing point, in order to assess how the waves were breaking and if a landing looked possible close up, we retreated a short way to organise ourselves for an attempt.

I moved up to the prow of the RIB, and Angus skilfully manoeuvred the boat into position whist Pete and Bob did their best to stabilise the platform for me to make the leap. At the first opportunity, Angus powered the RIB hard in and I stood on the prow of the boat ready to jump. As the swell took us up the rock, I focussed on my spot, went to push off the boat, but it fell away beneath me as the swell subsided. There was nothing to push off but I was committed and fell head first into the sea, without even touching Rockall!

Fortunately, I did not hit the rock and the swell was kind, pulling me away from the wall rather than slamming me into it. I was quickly plucked from the maelstrom by Bob and Pete. Angus decided we needed to bail out the boat, so we headed back to Orca 3, where everyone thought we'd given up. But no, a quick turnabout saw us motoring towards Rockall again. During the return to the rock, I moved in behind Bob for his attempt. To my surprise, however, on the re-approach to the landing point Bob indicated that I should have another go; a decision for which I am extremely grateful as it meant that I got to land and was able to continue my reconnaissance. If Bob had taken his spot and landed, I may not have had the opportunity of a second attempt and would then have not had the first-hand knowledge that proved so crucial in the planning and execution of the later expedition, nor would I have had the kudos of having landed, which I'm sure went some way to helping secure further sponsorship and press interest for the main expedition.

Reproduced with permission Michael Schofield

I moved to the prow again. This time we cleared all possible obstacles from my path, even attempting to untie the painter at the nose so that I did not get caught in it. Angus brought us in close again, I could her him revving the engine high as we noted the timing of the swell and the waves. He powered in when the swell was high, and I remember having one of those moments of complete clarity and focus, I could see the landing point, I knew I could make the jump, I just needed some luck. All three of the guys behind me were shouting for me to jump but I felt the swell ebb and I sensed that the next rise would suck us in closer and carry us a tad higher. It did, and I jumped. Landing hard, the water fell away and I heard the engine of the tender working to keep the guys safe and take them away from the surf. Instinct then kicked in, I knew from reading accounts of previous landings and watching footage that it was not unheard of to land and then be swept off immediately. The trick was to climb hard and fast as soon as you made contact with the rock, to get above the distinct horizontal crack above the landing point, and hopefully the high point of the waves. Only then could you relax a little, regain your breath, and focus for the climb that lay ahead.

I made the dash upwards, and once I had my breath back I started on the long traverse around the rock following the horizontal crack, which is much wider and deeper than it looks from afar, constantly reminding myself to take care in choosing good foot and hand holds as I was not tied on. I was quickly aware that the gloves I was wearing were preventing me from properly feeling the rock and perhaps limiting my hold and so I instinctively decided that I would not use them on the descent. Most of the traverse went smoothly, with the rock being predominantly very coarse and grippy with some large 'thank god' holds in key locations; although there is one slight overhang which requires some confidence and upper body strength, and a little bit of tricky route finding towards the end, before you emerge onto the long sloped scramble up to the summit. The second section was comparatively easy, with limited exposure, lots of features, including an old karabiner clipped through a natural loop weathered into the rock, and at a reasonably safe angle. The holds varied between bomb-proof and slim, but the coarseness of the rock provided decent grip, and I made good progress. After what seemed like half an hour of climbing, but in reality was probably ten minutes, I was there, on the summit ridge; just me, a few birds and the shell of the light beacon.

Although there appear to be a number of route options, including heading straight for the summit, or working back round to the end of Hall's Ledge, I knew that the nearest refuge and rest point was the West end of the summit ridge, where I could sit astride the ridge if necessary and catch my breath before moving on; bearing in mind that the whole climb was unprotected and I was now over fifteen metres above the sea. Looking down, I was surprised to see that Bob was still on the tender and assumed that he must have attempted to land and failed or been unable to get close enough, as I had previously thought that he would have moved to land as soon as possible after I was clear of the landing point. From my brief rest stop on the ridge, I moved to the summit, and without looking up heard cheers from the tender and the horn of Orca 3 being blown in celebration. I had made it to the top of Rockall at around 1600 hours, and the only folk who weren't happy were the gannets and guillemots that I disturbed with my arrival.

Reproduced with permission Michael Schofield

Having 'summited', my next task was to move down to Hall's Ledge, just below the summit, in order to get a sense of its true size and topography, check the condition of the anchors that Greenpeace had left in situ fifteen years earlier, take some photographs for my own records and for sponsors, and in order to haul up a dry sack full of basic kit, ropes and a bottle of Abhainn Dearg whisky. I had also hoped to bring up the empty whisky barrel which was to be subsequently filled and auctioned in support of Help for Heroes, but despite attempting to lift it by myself, both with ropes tied around it and inside a large holdall, its combined weight, the friction of the rope over the coarse rock, and the drag of the sea meant that I failed.

My original plan had been to use the light rope I had carried up with me to haul up a heavier rope, with which I would then pull up the kit bag and barrel. Unfortunately this had been lost in translation somewhere and the light rope was tied on to the kit bag by the support boat. Pulling the dry bag through the water was not too difficult, although the distance that it had been dropped into the sea could have been reduced. However, when it came time to pull the bag up the shear East face of Rockall, the friction between the rope and the rock was immense, especially as the edge of the rock from the face to the ledge was at a sharp angle where the rope changed direction. Even using my entire body weight to pull back along with all my leg and arm strength, I could not significantly move the bag which weighed no more than twenty kilogrammes, not helped by the slipperiness imparted to the rope by the guano that covers the rock.

This was my first lesson from this reconnaissance, the gear would have to go into the water nearer to the rock face in order to reduce energy expended hauling it through the water. I also needed to reduce the friction between the rock and the rope, perhaps lift from a higher angle in order to reduce the angle of transition, and finally, I would have to devise some kind of pulley or ratchet system, perhaps with a winch, as it was obvious that even with reduced friction in the system, I would still tire before I had hauled up all my kit, let alone dealt with the RockPod.

By this time, it was obvious that Bob had decided not to attempt a landing, but I was unable to ascertain why until I returned to the tender as the wind and breaking waves severely reduced the ability to communicate by shouting alone; I would need a radio for the expedition proper, in order to communicate with both Orca 3 and the tenders. Angus returned to Orca 3 and came back to the rock with what looked like a small bin. As I peered around the edge of the rock to see what he was up to, there was a loud explosion, and thankfully it quickly dawned on me that he'd fired a rocket in my general direction! I ducked as it whistled past my head, dragging behind it a light line, with which I hauled up the heavier rope as originally planned. The wind dropped long enough for the shot to be perfectly placed and for Angus and myself to exchange laughter and not a few swear words before getting back to work. I later found out that Angus had never used one of these before, so perhaps it was beginner's luck that his shot was dead on.

I retrieved the line and started to haul. Pulling the first pack about half way up the steep East face, it quickly became obvious that the bag was going no higher due to this rope also slipping through my hands. Angus decided that he should try and pull it up with the tender. He proceeded around to the other side of the rock, to the point where I had climbed up, and I threw down the line. The system worked well, except for the inability to communicate swiftly enough to get him to stop pulling once the bag was aloft. I was jerked to the ground while attempting to hold onto the pack and badly jarred my knee. Anyway the pack was up.

Photos taken, and the first 'Tweet' and Facebook update sent from Rockall via Bob's satellite phone, I was requested to return to Orca 3 as the weather was turning for the worse earlier than forecast. I'd been on Rockall for about an hour, but with all the action it felt like ten minutes. I was left with one dry sack to retrieve, but very little in the way of ropes. Deciding to tie my static abseiling line to the remains of the haul line, I lowered the bag over the edge to the waiting tender. This got caught on the jagged rock below, so I retrieved it and decided, with much shouting to the tender, that the best option was to throw down the line for them to retrieve followed by the bag. Fortunately the bag sailed high and wide, despite its weight, and made it to the ocean. Unsurprisingly the climbing rope sank and so the tender had to come close in to the rock to retrieve the line. The bag and its contents were hauled aboard. Surprisingly, the bottle of whisky within had remained intact despite all the action!

All that remained on Rockall was me. I down-climbed the same route that I had taken up but without gloves, and in some respects this was much easier than the climb up. I took a minor detour and had to back track, but otherwise it went well and I made it to the surf line. Taking a moment to decide which direction to jump, the decision was made for me! In one last act of dominance, a wave came from the side and slapped me off the face of Rockall. I hit the water hard, but again my equipment did its job and I swam as quickly as I could to get out of the surf and re-join the tender.

Reproduced with permission Michael Schofield

Once back on Orca 3, there was lots of congratulating and hand shaking before I took a seat and a moment to take in what I had achieved. Very few people have seen Rockall let alone set foot on it, and many of those who had landed didn't make it to the top. To have visited, landed and summited, albeit briefly, was a fantastic feeling. However, we had to move quickly as the weather was turning, which was why I hadn't stayed on the rock overnight as hoped. Everything, including the tender, was pulled aboard, lashed down and we headed back east towards St. Kilda. I managed to get eight or nine hours sleep on the journey back, and awoke to a ghost ship in Village Bay; everyone else on board was sleeping. There had been much sea sickness overnight as it was a rough crossing which I had fortunately missed. When Angus did eventually wake up, he proclaimed that he wasn't going back out to Rockall for a very long time!

Upon reflection, the reconnaissance of 2012 to Rockall was a key piece in the jigsaw of putting together the main expedition in 2014. Without going to the rock, I would have fallen into the trap of assuming that everything I'd heard and read was true, taken poor decisions about some key pieces of equipment, and would have been heading out there hoping, rather than knowing, that my plan was going to work. I spent the sail back to shore from Rockall that year, when not sleeping, writing notes and lists of tasks I needed to complete, and skills I needed to gain before heading out again. I decided that I needed to think more 'marine' and take less of a climbing approach. This meant different ropes, knots, and perhaps a breeches buoy.

I had noted that hauling my bag back up the groove in the rock was much easier than up the East face, and decided that I should investigate hauling techniques used on big walls and in mountain rescue. I needed a mechanical advantage, and that meant winching. I also needed to be stronger and have more muscle stamina, which I had time to gain through training, but I also needed specific gloves for hauling on ropes when they were wet and slippery with guano. I had confirmed that I did not need extra grips on my boots, that the Greenpeace bolts were still in good condition, that my kit had to go into the water as close to the rock as possible. It also had to be grouped in smaller, lighter bundles and probably in barrels as the coarse rock had cut through my dry bags.

In addition to equipment and my own fitness and techniques for getting my kit onto Hall's Ledge, the trip had confirmed that the new boat, Orca 3, owned and operated by Angus Campbell of Kilda Cruises and Atlantic Marine Services was the perfect vessel for the job. I was asked a number of times during the course of organising this expedition why I did not charter a cheaper yacht, with less fuel requirements and hence a lower cost. To me, the answer was simple: the success or failure of Rockall Solo was, to a greater or lesser extent, decided by speed and weather. Although more expensive, a motorised vessel taking fifteen hours to reach Rockall, as opposed to approximately sixteen or more hours on a sailing boat allowed me to fit my landing into a shorter weather window.

Additionally, Orca 3 is much more manoeuvrable on site than a yacht would be, and importantly as a catamaran is much more stable. Finally, her speed meant that she could run ahead of the weather, as she did on our return from Rockall in 2012, should things turn bad, therefore ensuring, as much as is possible, the safety of her crew and me. I believed, therefore, that the extra cost of fuel was justified. I just had to find a way of paying for it! After my return from Rockall that summer, I had to have a good hard think about the future of the expedition. I wanted to go back more than ever, but would I find the money?

There's a difficult balance to be struck with expedition sponsors. Ideally one would plan a challenge that you could afford yourself, didn't have to rely on corporate funding, and therefore had no obligation to seek media coverage in order for these companies to realise a return for their outlay. On the other hand, unless you're very wealthy, no expedition of this type or one which requires a lot of investment would ever go ahead. This has always been the case: even Shackleton had his corporate sponsors after whom life boats were named, and whose products he plugged during his post-expedition talks.

From experience, my advice is to be careful who you choose to partner with and what you promise them in return. My approach, at first, was that I needed kit and equipment which I could either try to get hard cash to buy, or I could approach the manufacturer who already has the kit in storage, waiting to go in the shops in a warehouse somewhere. It's easier to get the kit than the money, particularly if you can be seen in photos using it, and have somewhere prominent to display the company's logo (such as a RockPod). Some companies I talked to had a million questions; some even had application forms to fill in. Unless you're desperate, I wouldn't bother with those; if they're hard to deal with at the start, they're only going to be harder to deal with in the long term.

However, at some point you are going to need hard cash, and in my case it was to pay the boatman. Money is much more difficult to obtain. I tried a few of the expedition grant making trusts, but Rockall Solo didn't really fit into any of the narrow pigeon holes that they define. I wrote to and spoke to a number of large local firms, some of whom I had personal introductions to or associations with; no joy. They didn't see the benefit to them of paying me to go and sit on a rock – they just didn't get it.

The best sponsors are those who just 'get it', and by that I mean understand the concept, quickly see the possibilities for media coverage and therefore brand exposure, and are therefore only too eager to give you what you need. My experience would suggest that these companies also tend to ask for relatively little in return, just best endeavours to get their logo seen and a mention here and there in the press or on your blog; the power of the re-Tweet is amazing. Similarly, there were individuals who understood the idea of the expedition, thought it was great and only had excitement for what I was attempting to achieve. Others will have a million questions and still not understand your motivations (even if you can fully explain them, which I couldn't). In my pursuit of sponsorship, I started to think along the lines, "You either get it, or you don't". If they didn't, I thanked them politely by email, and moved on. There are a lot of companies to get through and some of them will understand your madness. That's the nub really: it becomes a job trying to obtain sponsorship, and it will take up a lot of your time.

As an example, my biggest financial sponsor, Calor, immediately understood the concept; or at least my contact there did and he was listened to. I was introduced to them by the World Liquid Petroleum Gas Association (WLPGA). I managed to get the WLPGA involved by thinking outside the box: around Christmas time in 2012 I had nowhere near enough funding and was considering cancelling the 2013 attempt as I needed to let Kilda Cruises know as soon as possible if I was going ahead, so that they knew whether or not to block book the time I needed.

After a few glasses of wine one evening, I had an epiphany, and searched the web for anyone called Rockall, which came up with the President of the WLPGA, James Rockall. I wrote to him, along with about forty other people called Rockall. James saw the opportunity (no-one else did!), and came straight back to me. He could see the obvious links between their campaign 'LPG Exceptional Energy', which aimed to promote the use of LPG in remote areas, and my need for a reliable and clean fuel source for cooking while on the rock. He said that they were on board, asked how much I needed, and that they would introduce me to some of their clients.

Calor backed me for the first attempt, and when I went back to them cap in hand to ask whether they might consider part funding a second attempt, they paid for it all and asked for nothing more apart from that I kept doing what I was already doing. The perfect sponsors. I needed to use LPG for cooking, which they supplied along with a stove so that I could demonstrate, in a unique scenario, how versatile LPG is. They also gave me some branded clothing, the same as that which their delivery drivers are issued, therefore incurring no additional cost, on to which I had other logos embroidered and which became my expedition 'uniform'. WLPGA and Calor also stepped in towards the end of the expedition, when I lost kit barrels and food in a storm, to offer unsolicited help towards the cost of getting additional supplies out to me if I wanted. Finally, when I ran over budget due to a miscalculation on my part regarding the day charter of the boat, they happily paid the extra funds that I needed.

Other sponsors were not so easy to deal with. I did end up filling in some applications for funding, and was successful, which is how I know that these companies will be on at you to push their name hard in all your blogs and Tweets, want higher profile logo positions than their contribution justified when compared to other sponsors, and will be on the phone or email all the time wanting to know what more you can give them. Again, my experience is that if they believe they're so big that they need a form, they'll believe they're your biggest sponsor. If you really have to take this route, deal with them, otherwise look for other options because their demands will only distract from the whole reason you were talking to them in the first place: to organise and pay for an expedition.

CHAPTER IV

THE ROCKPOD

I made the decision to go for a rigid shelter rather than a tent or something similar at an early stage of the planning process, a decision which was dictated by the weather conditions on Rockall, and also by using the experience of the previous parties who have stayed on Rockall for any length of time, Tom McLean and Greenpeace. Tom used a homemade plywood box tied down with nylon rope, and Greenpeace used a bespoke Kevlar reinforced fibre-glass pod, which I understand they had previously used on various protests around the world.

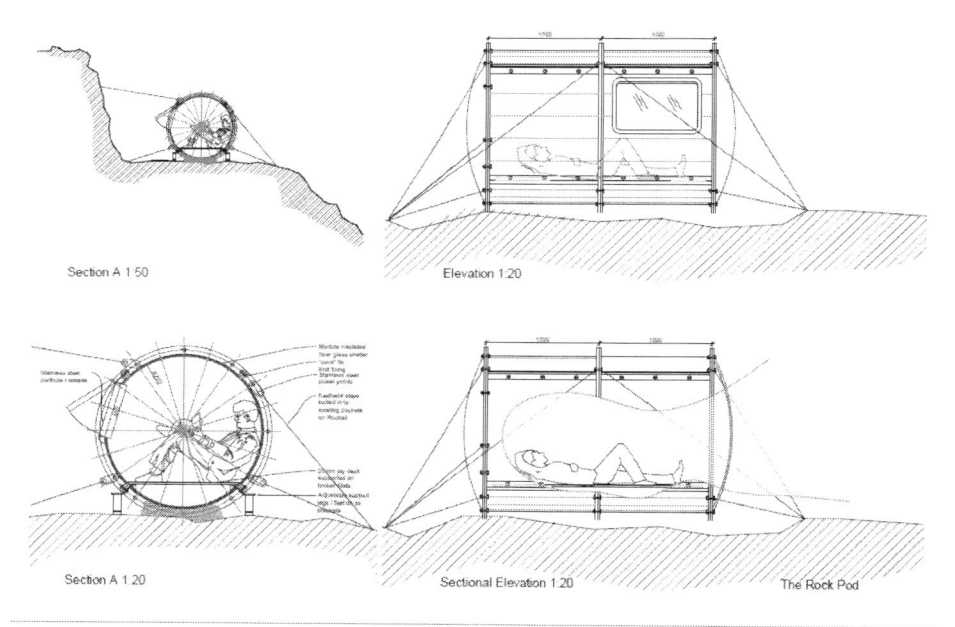

Initial design drawings for The RockPod – Andrew Bell

My budget didn't spread to the equivalent of Greenpeace's pod, I couldn't borrow it as it had been crushed by the Norwegian government, and I couldn't afford a helicopter to lift it on to Rockall. I also wanted something more substantial and stronger than a plywood box! A friend of mine, Andy Bell, is an architect, and in April 2009 he kindly put some drawings together of a bespoke shelter for me, based on a smaller version of the Greenpeace pod, which he christened 'The RockPod'. I had this costed up by a couple of specialist companies, including one that made the pod for the Breitling Orbiter balloon, and who do work for NASA. Even just paying for materials, it was still too expensive, so I started hunting for a suitable object to modify. Secretly I was quite pleased, as I liked the idea of an eccentric, 'Heath Robinson', homemade shelter, rather than a hyper professional super-technical one.

Having considered and rejected various options including a small shipping container unit, various porta-cabin type buildings and an urban air quality monitoring station, I finally came across a water bowser at some road works in London on my way home from taking part in the Marathon des Sables. It took a while to track down the manufacturer as most of the hire firms I contacted were somewhat reticent about telling me where they sourced them from. Finally, I managed to contact Trailer Engineering, who had a proto-type of a new design which they said I could have for free if I collected it from Birmingham, which I duly did.

Once the new bowser was home, in September 2011, I had to go about converting it to its new use. I had already agreed with Lewmar that they would supply the marine hatches I would need. I had previously decided on a square access hatch, but as luck would have it, their largest round hatch matched exactly the moulding on the top of the bowser, so I ordered that instead. This hatch was only fitted with handles on the inside, and as I would need to be able to open and close the hatch from the outside as well, Lewmar sent me technical drawings for a metal internal handle spindle that would link the handles when mounted inside and outside the hatch. They did not at that time manufacture this spindle, but my friend Jamie asked a colleague to make it, and shortly afterwards two shiny new aluminium components arrived which perfectly fitted the hatches and handles. The side hatch, which was not strictly necessary, but meant that I would not be stuck looking at the sky if I got pod-bound for a few days, is designed for a flat surface with a tolerance of just a couple of millimetres. This created difficulties fitting it to the curved wall of the pod, and meant that I had to cut a recess into the wall and remould the plastic around the hatch using the off cuts and a heat gun. The hatches arrived in October 2011, and the conversion of the water bowser could then begin in earnest.

The hatches were fixed with stainless steel bolts, and had both a neoprene gasket and marine grade silicone sealant around them to keep the water out. Similarly, the openings for the bowser's previous incarnation were sealed with silicone. I also installed a Lewmar deck vent, for those times when the weather didn't allow me to open the hatches for ventilation, and a target level to help level the pod once on Rockall.

My next job was to attach the fixing points to the side and top of the RockPod, from which ratchet straps (the system used and proved by Greenpeace on Rockall) would attach to fixing points on the rock left in place by Greenpeace. As part of my recce trip in 2012, I had inspected the condition of these fixings: they looked like new and were all still well fixed in place; but I would be taking back-ups in case any came loose during my stay. The one tonne rated fixing points were supplied by William Hacket Chains, and again were bolted on with stainless steel bolts and back plates, with silicone sealant to fill any gaps. I then stuck a number of self-adhesive grip pads around the 'deck' of the pod to assist climbing and moving about on it, as the surface was shiny and very slippery when wet.

Internally, I fitted a plastic floor to level the convex moulded base, supported at the edges with off-cuts of plastic pipe as legs and insulated below with expanding foam and reflective foil. The walls and 'ceiling' were insulated with spray-on foam by Foamspray Technologies, and this was in turn sealed with a rubberised paint to provide a cleanable surface. Externally, and following the first round of winch testing, I adapted the original 'design' by filling the exterior of the concave base with more expanding foam and fitting a plywood base, as in testing the recess caught on rocks as it was being winched. In addition, I fitted two additional lifting points much lower down on the RockPod, specifically for winching it up Rockall and also as a result of issues encountered during testing. The end result, more by evolution than design, was a strong, rigid, waterproof, but relatively light weight shelter (circa 150-180kg) which was designed to float, and although Spartan inside, would, I was confident, protect me from everything the summer Atlantic could throw at me.

Reproduced with permission Michael Schofield

I then turned to testing. In December 2012, on a very cold day, the first job was to check that the pod floated as my plan was to tow it from Orca 3 to

Rockall using a tender. The Seagull Trust in Ratho operate a dry dock on the canal where they mend barges, and which is fitted with a small crane. They very kindly agreed to let me use the crane to lift the pod into the canal. Using their facility, I could check that my design was strong enough to be lifted by a crane and was stable while being hoisted, as it would have to be to get it off the boat. I was a tad nervous as the RockPod broke through the ice into the murky water, but it did float and was surprisingly very stable. I avoided the temptation to see it if would self-right with me in it, much to the disappointment of my goading friend and glamorous assistant Dan, but I did stand astride the deck, rocking the pod violently to see if it would tip over and then, once confident that it wouldn't, I got inside, while it was still afloat, to check if there were any leaks, which thankfully there were not.

We then moved venue to the hidden, but publicly open crag behind the Edinburgh International Climbing Area (EICA), which happily is also in Ratho. There I met up with Fraser Macdonald and Stevie Young, both rope rescue instructors at the National Rope Rescue Centre in Edinburgh and owners of Summit Rescue. These were the guys to teach me the specialist skills, over and above my existing climbing experience, required to enable me to winch and lower the RockPod over a cliff on my own.

This was my first opportunity to use the Portable Winch, and to see how strong and easy to use it actually was. I had initially intended to use a locking cam on a pulley to feed the rope from the winch through, so that I could lock off the system if I had any problems or became tired. I had also planned to use a single line to lift the pod up the rock. Stevie and Fraser immediately suggested that I use a two point system with the rope fixed at one end at the top of the crag, going down and feeding through a pulley at the 'nose' of the pod, and then going back up to the winch. In this way, the winch would only be lifting half the weight of the pod, as the other half would be taken by the fixed end of the rope. They also introduced me to a piece of hardware made by Petzl called an ID, which instead of having a toothed cam to lock onto the rope, had a smooth releasable one, which overcame the issue of not being able to release the pod and lower it back down the rock or onto the safety line if I needed to, when the system was loaded. The RockPod was easily lowered down the face using the ID, which had an inbuilt safety feature, so if I accidently let go of it, the cam would automatically lock onto the rope preventing a fall.

Once part way down the face, we commenced with the first short winch, which immediately revealed problems: whenever the RockPod hit a feature on the face, the nose would dig in and tail would lift out from the rock, forcing the nose harder against the rock and making it almost impossible to lift. Added to this, the pulley attached to the single strap running across the nose of the pod would slip to one side as soon as an obstruction was encountered, so that the shelter would be being lifted from a corner rather than straight on. We also discovered that by far the most difficult point in the lift was the transition from vertical to horizontal at the top of the cliff, as the rope would be running at a sharp angle over the edge as the pod rose up, adding yet more friction into an already heavily loaded system. We completed the short winch, and after a few slightly longer ones I felt that I had learnt enough about the system I would use to haul the RockPod up Rockall, but I had also seen that I needed to make some modifications to the pod specifically to make the winching process smoother.

Primarily, I needed to rethink the position of the winching points. It was apparent that I would need to fit additional lifting points lower down near the base of the pod and set back from the front, in order that the RockPod tipped back from the rock face, the nose of the pod was lifted away from the cliff, and only the tail dragged up the rock, so that it would more easily overcome any features on the face on which it would otherwise get caught. I also need to have a fixed central lifting point for the winch line and pulley to attach to, in order to avoid the tendency to tilt to one side when it got caught on even the smallest feature.

The Portable Winch had proved to be the perfect tool for the job; it easily hauled the RockPod up the cliff, stalling only when the friction in the system became too great and I failed to increase the revs quickly enough, or when the RockPod got caught on a larger feature which required Stevie, who was hanging alongside the pod on the cliff to guide it up, to intervene and physically push the pod off the feature. Crucially, there were far more rock features on the cliff face in Ratho than on the East face of Rockall and it was complicated by a vertical feature which ran the whole height of the face, which does not exist on Rockall, and which imparted yet more drag on the pod as it rose up the cliff. If I could devise a complete system with which I could easily lift the pod up the quarry cliff, then the lift on Rockall would be significantly easier.

Reproduced with permission Michael Schofield

In the spring of 2013, and having made the required modifications to the RockPod, including fitting the two lifting points to the pod, obtaining a pair of shorter lifting straps so that the pulley was fixed centrally in front of the pod as it was winched, and additionally fitting wheels under the nose in the hope that these would aid lifting the nose over any obstacles, I returned to the quarry and met again with Stevie and Fraser. The aim of the day was simple: to check whether the alterations I'd made to the lifting points and system had the desired effect, and whether the winch could now lift the RockPod more easily. I again started with a short lift to ascertain whether there were any major issues, and then we went full a full height lift up the crag.

Both went well, although the wheels tended to catch a little on features before rolling over them, but the issues of the pod's nose digging in and slipping to one side had been overcome. However, the real problem with this test came when we continued the winch up to the top and the pod was pulled over the transition point. The wheels caught hard and would not lift up and over the edge without interference from a couple of us physically lifting the pod over the edge. Although the transition from the eastern cliff face of Rockall onto Hall's Ledge would be much more gradual, it was obvious that the wheels would have to come off. In any case, the RockPod seemed to me to be coming up the face, using the new lifting points, with the nose away from the wall as planned and the previous test day had demonstrated that it coped well with the transition when there were no wheels fitted. The wheels came off the next morning.

With the bolt holes sealed where the wheels had been removed, I was confident that the system we had devised would work well on Rockall. The only phase of the landing I had not practiced was the transition of the pod from the sea to the vertical on the rock face, but I reasoned that the Orca 3 crew in the tender should be able to keep it from flipping, assuming suitable sea conditions to allow me to land, while I winched a little faster at that point in the lift. I felt I was ready to go in a few months' time.

CHAPTER V

2013

It was the 29th May 2013, and I found myself again sitting at Lickisto Blackhouse on the Isle of Harris, but my situation was very different from the year before:

After the successful reconnaissance in 2012, happily, the financial sponsors I had lined up then had agreed to roll their pledges of funding over to 2013, but that had still left me short of the total sum I needed to pay for the boat charters and various pieces of equipment that I had been unable to negotiate for free. Having sent out hundreds of emails to potential funders in the autumn of 2012, including pledges of support, I was still short of over half the total amount required to pay for the boat charters at the start and the end of the main expedition and for equipment that I had not already secured. Now into the third year of attempting to get the expedition off the ground, I was really pushing hard and asking every contact I had if they would consider recommending to their contacts that they support the expedition. Funding the expedition had become a full-time job.

After my return from Rockall in the summer of 2012, I had to have a good hard think about the future of the expedition. I wanted to go back more than ever, but would I find the money? With some judicious rethinking, re-planning, and re-budgeting, I managed to reduce the overall budget for the expedition by a third going forward into 2013. This was now the bare bones figure for the expedition, and a high proportion of these costs were boat charter and fuel (an estimated, unfixed cost that far ahead of departure!). However, since my return, I had been looking at reducing costs further, and it was with this in mind that I started a new round of emails, asking for further goods and services instead of cash. This had been the most successful tactic up to this point, as companies have products they will loan or donate in return for PR, and others can provide their services free of charge, at no huge cost to themselves.

By the start of 2013, I had all the funding I needed in place, and commitments from various equipment suppliers for the remaining gear I needed. Additionally, Mark Beaumont, knowing about my funding issues, had suggested that I enter the competition for the inaugural Kukri Adventure Scholarship, which was an adventure supporting fund aiming to give successful applicants partial funding for their expeditions. I duly applied and submitted my application video online, and was surprised to be short listed. This meant travelling down to the Royal Geographical Society in London, a place I knew well, and making a presentation to the judging panel which included Mark, Kukri management and Sarah Outen. The announcement of the results was the same day and I was amazed that I had been awarded part of the fund, along with several other 'adventurers' including Niall Iain Macdonald who was planning to row solo across the North Atlantic from New York to Stornoway around the same time that I hoped to also be in the North Atlantic but stationary on Rockall.

Reproduced with permission of Kukri

Up to this point, and in an effort to create media interest in the expedition in order to demonstrate to potential sponsors that I was worthy of supporting, I had been contacting various newspapers, television channels, programme makers and production companies with a view to getting press coverage and perhaps making a documentary while I was on the rock. There had been some early interest from the regional press in Scotland, and the Scottish Sun had accompanied me in 2012. Now I had the promise of a blog for The Guardian newspaper while on Rockall, and they also set up a special section on their website dedicated to the expedition, which they planned to populate with articles and interviews as the expedition progressed. This support along with growing interest from the producers of the BBC's 'One Show' meant that my media profile grew rapidly through the latter stages of the winter and into spring 2013.

However, I quickly discovered that media interest can be a double edged sword. Having had no previous experience or guidance in this field, I was determined to milk it for all it was worth and I spread myself very thinly, attempting to make myself available for all reporters and interviews on their timescales, either in person or over the telephone, bearing in mind that I still had a full time job and a young family that needed my time too.

A week or two before my planned departure, 'The One Show' sent someone to interview me at home and work in order to provide some background to the piece they were putting together. This was really the start of some immense pressure from the media in the final two weeks build up to the expedition which not only distracted me from the task at hand and the reason they wanted to speak to me, the expedition, but also started to become very stressful and affect me both physically and mentally. There were seemingly constant telephone calls and emails, not only from the media, but also sponsors, and I had final pieces of organisation to complete. I couldn't wait for the expedition to get started so that I could get away from all these extraneous demands and get on with the project.

Once back on Harris it didn't stop. I was met off the ferry by a reporter that I had previously taken a particular dislike to because of his general attitude and the fact that he had printed some very misleading articles in the run up to the expedition both in 2012 and 2013. 'The One Show' had various things they wanted to film and interviews they wanted to get before departure, which I didn't mind at all and wanted to do, but along with everything else, could really have done without; and on top of that there was a Guardian photographer who wanted to get some shots of me with the RockPod, which again I wanted to do but time was against me. In the end, one of the shots Murdo MacLeod took in the short window that I was able to give him was listed in The Guardian's portraits of the year.

Reproduced with permission Murdo Macleod/The Guardian

So it was that I was in Harris in very much not the right frame of mind for setting off on a potentially sixty day solo expedition to the middle of nowhere. Looking back at photographs of this time for this book, I can see the stress and worry clearly etched on my face. My friend Jamie had driven up with me in order to help me organize my equipment, help with the loading of the boat and then drive the van back to Edinburgh, assuming I successfully landed. Having carried out some minor final checks of kit at the campsite, which was off the beaten track and an ideal place to disappear and hide from the media, I filled my twenty five litre water jerry cans from their tap and prepared as best I could for departure the next day.

The weather that day, like the previous few days, had been one of contrasts: it had been calm and clear, with a still sea and no breeze, ostensibly perfect conditions for landing on Rockall, but I was stuck with the memory of my past few days of preparation as being hectic, rushing around the island to do some last minute filming and interviews, and speaking to various people in the team about the challenges and issues ahead. I was not in the right place mentally.

That evening I met with Angus Campbell and his in-house forecaster, Jeevan Toor, to go over the most recent weather buoy data and the weather and swell forecasts for the next few days, whilst again being filmed. We had to think long and hard whether the window we had to get me and all my kit out to and then onto Rockall would be big enough. We knew that the swell may be a deciding factor, and in the end it was. It looked like we'd have a brief window of near perfect landing conditions on the Friday morning in two days' time. The price we would pay for that window was going to be one hell of a journey out to Rockall in big waves and high winds. Feeling that it was a price worth paying, and with a lack of other suitable windows in the next few days, when I had the boat chartered, I decided to go for it.

First thing the next morning I was down at the jetty at Leverburgh with Jamie and the van and we loaded up Orca 3. The crew would comprise Angus MacDonald and Angus Smith again, Peter Macdonald, Alastair Morrison, both Kilda Cruises staff, Ruari Beaton who had not made it out the previous year, along with the three man 'One Show' crew and myself. I was very aware as we pulled out of Leverburgh and I waved goodbye to Jamie, Severin from the Guardian (with whom I'd struck up a friendship), and various other television and newspaper reporters, that I'd been feeling somewhat lost for the last couple of days, sitting and waiting to hear if we were going to Rockall, with no control over that or the demands of the previous media commitments I'd made; but now I was able to wrestle some control back, even if it was just doing what I needed to do, organising and checking my gear, and preparing for the landing the next day.

We arrived on site at Rockall, in the dark as planned, at around 0100, after leaving Leverburgh on Harris at 1130 the previous morning. We then circled for a couple of hours, waiting for first light in order to assess the sea state and the condition of the rock. Orca 3 moved in close to Rockall as dawn broke; there were more sea birds on Hall's Ledge and scattered around the summit than the previous year, but there appeared to be less guano. However, the striking factor was the swell; hitting Rockall from the West, exactly where I didn't want it to be: there is a small step in the cliff on the Western flank which is the 'normal' landing platform, and is the point from where you commence the fast vertical scramble to safety out of the swell zone, before traversing across the Western face and back to reach the summit.

The swell ebbed and flowed strongly, hitting exactly the point where I would, like the previous year, have to jump. It hurtled three or four metres up the side of the rock, well above the usual safety mark, and then plunged four or five metres into a deep hole below the step. This created a potential fall, before being able to reach safety, of almost ten metres onto the skirt of rock around the base of Rockall that is usually submerged in calmer conditions, and a hole into which the RIB, its crew and any kit on board would be sucked, flipped and then scraped back up the rock face.

The previous year I remembered looking at the landing point and being overwhelmingly confident of making the jump and clambering to safety. This time it was different; the combination of such a short time to reach safety, which would mean climbing to a higher point up the face in a shorter time, and then the exposure as the sea fell away below, just did not feel right. Angus Smith, the skipper, took me aside and made it clear that he was not happy about me leaving the Orca to attempt a landing in these conditions, nor was he keen to endanger his crew on the RIBs. In the end, he thankfully took the inevitable decision out of my hands.

Looking back, I feel that the fates were playing their cards well: after the rigors of the media interest in the previous few days and weeks, I was not in the right frame of mind to be starting an expedition of this scale. I now think that if I had landed successfully and got all my gear up onto the rock that day, I would have faced a completely different and dark mental battle for at least the first few days of my occupation. In addition, on the way out to Rockall both Angus Smith and Ruari, both experienced boat builders, had expressed concern that the paint on the inside of the RockPod was still giving off volatile organic compound fumes (VOCs) after I had hurriedly rushed to get the construction finished in time for departure. Everything had conspired against me; it had been decided. This was not my year.

I said at the time, and I believed, that like a mountain summit, Rockall would be there another day. It wasn't going anywhere. While it was obviously difficult to turn my back on the rock, and to be sailing away, running before the weather, I was confident that the correct decision was made by Angus that day. With time on my hands during the return journey to Harris, I watched back the footage that The One Show team had shot of the sea state at Rockall and looked at the pictures taken while we were there and they all reaffirmed that it was not to be the day.

After the reconnaissance expedition the previous year, I had spent some time on the return journey reflecting on what I had learnt from it and writing lists of actions moving forward; I did the same again now. After the weather that day, I wanted to investigate the costs of helicopter charter, despite the purist in me wanting to land by boat. I needed more accurate weather forecasting, and I should practice the transition of the RockPod from water to rock during the winching. I realised how important my mental fitness and morale were going to be; I would need to come back fit and focussed, which meant less demands from the media. I needed high-octane music on my iPod and some energy drinks prior to the landing in order to get pumped up and alert after the long journey to the rock, and I would need life insurance!

Jamie met me off the boat and we quietly packed the van back up and limped home. I contacted my sponsors to let them know what had happened, and after some final media commitments, I put the expedition to bed and enjoyed a summer with my family that I had not expected to have.

CHAPTER VI

FOOD AND WATER

With regard to food, I had decided early on, from past experience, that boil in the bag military rations were going to be the best way forward for a number of reasons. My options were either these or freeze dried rations, which would be lighter and take up less space, but required fresh water to re-hydrate them, and really need to be heated to allow them to re-hydrate properly. I already had to take a huge amount of fresh water with me just for drinking as there is no supply on Rockall, and an additional supply to rehydrate my food would have been immense. In addition, and as happened, if my stove broke down or I lost fuel, I would struggle to re-hydrate the food at all. I also thought about bringing some fresh food with me for the start of the expedition, but reasoned that there was a contamination issue, and I may be mentally affected in the long term by wishing I'd tried to eek the fresh food out for longer.

Boil in the bag rations had several advantages: they could be eaten hot or cold, did not require extra water, did not dirty my pan while cooking, I could eat them out of the bags so didn't need a bowl, and perhaps most importantly they are sterile, which in a dirty, guano covered environment like Rockall was very important in order to avoid bowel issues. Morale wise, I know, from previous mountaineering expeditions and time spent with the military, that food becomes very important. In the rations, there is a good variety of meals, which in recent years have been greatly improved in texture and flavour (although I could live without the mushroom 'omelette'), and which provide a balanced range of fibre, protein, energy, etc. Furthermore, the ration packs had a defined average calorie amount, which meant that I could break them down evenly to ensure I was getting the sustenance that I needed.

Each normal military twenty four hour ration pack contains an average of 4,500 calories. This figure is so high as they have to sustain fit soldiers in very active pursuits for prolonged periods of time. The average man needs around 2,500 calories per day to live a normal reasonably active life style. I am not very big, and would not be particularly active, and so I reasoned that I could survive on an average of 2,250 calories (half a twenty four hour ration pack) each day. I may lose a bit of weight, but I planned for this by eating very well and drinking good ale in the run up to the expedition!

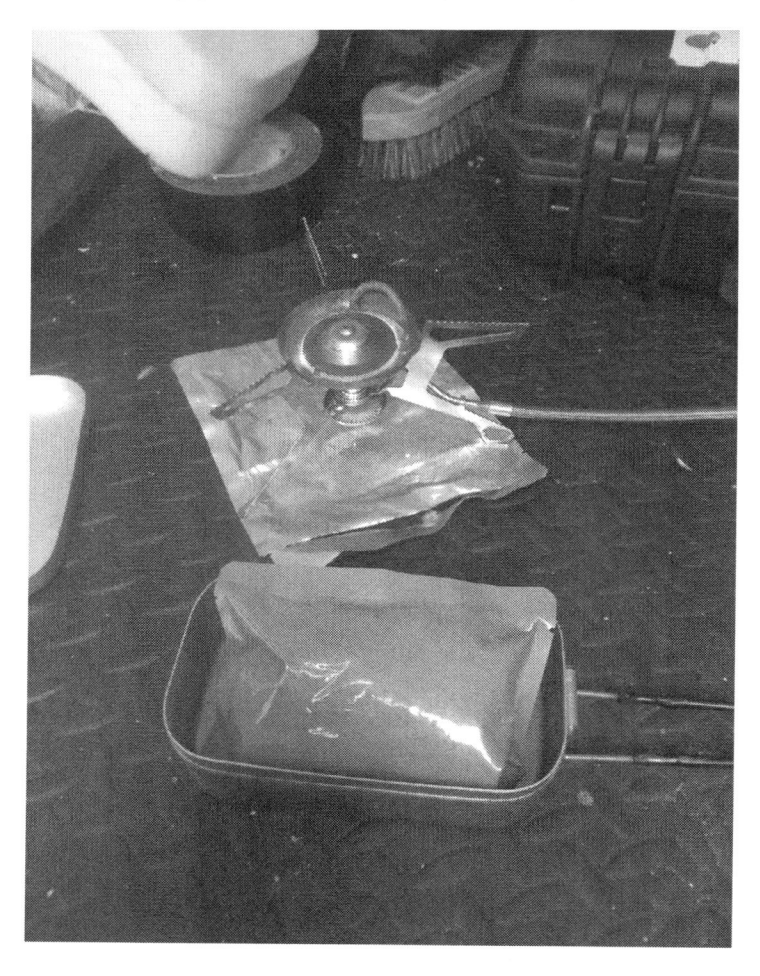

I did not plan my meal split before I left, thinking correctly that I would have time to get into a pattern once I was on Rockall. Initially, my division of the rations was a bit haphazard, but I quickly got into a daily routine, which depending on the particular menu, usually meant protein heavy on day one and next to no protein on day two. On day one breakfast, which was normally around 0900, was usually boil in the bag sausage, or bacon and beans with a cup of tea. I would have a coffee mid-morning, and lunch (around 1400) would be herb 'spread' (pate) on 'biscuits brown' with one piece of chocolate. In the evening I would have whatever hot meal was in the ration pack (usually pasta or stew) around 1900, with a mug of hot chocolate and a couple of chunks of chocolate before bed. I would drink water between meals, and had allowed myself a daily ration, including tea and coffee, of two and a half litres, although I had enough with me so that on hotter days I easily drank three litres with no issue.

Day two was never as nice as the first: breakfast would be 'fruit spread' (jam) in a tube on 'biscuits fruit' with a small pack of 'berry combo fruit grains' (fruit puree treats) and a cup of tea. Again, I would have coffee mid-morning, but only half a mug as there were only three sachets of coffee in each ration pack, and I would have used two the day before. Lunch was not great either: a tube of 'yeast extract' (Marmite) on an 'oatmeal block' (shortbread) which was never big enough, so I would have to swallow lumps of 'yeast extract' on their own to make sure I was getting all the calories, followed by a 'fruit and oats snack bar'. I'd often wash this down with an isotonic drink, orange or berry flavours, made with a sachet of powder that also came in the ration pack.

Supper on day two was always the wrong way around as I had to boil water for a sachet of instant soup, within which I heated whatever pudding came with that particular menu. I would then eat the pudding first, while it was hot, followed by the soup, then the final couple of chunks of chocolate I would have left from the five chunk bar which came in each ration pack. The tea was in a powdered 'instant white' form, and although I would not normally have sugar in tea or coffee at home, in order to ingest some additional calories I would have a standard ten gram sachet of white sugar in each hot drink. Excluding the chocolate, and in between meals I would either chew gum or eat boiled sweets, which also came in the ration packs. On this regime, I rarely felt hungry between meals and lost very little weight, only about seven pounds over the course of the expedition.

CHAPTER VII

2014 EXPEDITION DIARY

The journey to Harris was uneventful and went as planned. Pam and I stopped in briefly to see our friends Dan and Ann at their bed and breakfast, Strath Lodge in Glencoe, before heading on to Uig. Pam took over the driving at this stage as she wanted to practice driving such a large vehicle, over six metres long, on the narrow Highland roads. We reached Uig without issue around 1900 and got registered at the bed and breakfast before heading to the Ferry Inn for supper – a strange affair as we were told we couldn't eat in the bar as they were short staffed, so we went instead to the very quiet restaurant, whereupon the barman appeared three or four times with drinks, so could easily have brought our food back with him to the bar!

Freddie didn't sleep well as it was so light, dropping off around 2200 and waking again at 0600, which meant that neither of us got a good night's sleep either. Anyway, we were up, breakfasted and down at the ferry terminal on time and managed to collect the tickets for both round trips at the start and end of the expedition, which would make life a bit simpler for Jamie and Pam later on.

Freddie loved the ferry and was fascinated with being on a boat that cars and lorries could fit on. Pam managed the drive onto the ferry with no problems and we settled in for the journey across the Minch. None of us felt sick, it was a relatively calm day, but Freddie, forever exploring and going on adventures, slipped Pam's grasp and before she knew it, he had tumbled down four or five of the external steel steps. The first I knew of it was when I heard her scream his name and turned to see her dash down after him. When I arrived, she had him in her arms, he was crying and she was shaken, but fortunately his only injury was a bloody lip. Not a great start!

We arrived in Tarbert slightly late, owing to a delayed departure waiting for a latecomer to board, but that made no difference to us as we moseyed down to the Blackhouse campsite at Lickisto, and met up with Harvey who had injured his foot. Harvey's able assistant showed us to our yurt and we brought down most of our family kit in the wheelbarrows provided. Once settled, and having received an email from Angus Campbell the night before that departure looked good for Wednesday (the next day) we headed down to Leverburgh to see if Ruari was in at the Am Bothan Bunkhouse, which he wasn't, before heading up to the beach at Luskentyre as it was such a beautiful day and we wanted to spend as much family time together as we could.

Freddie played on the sand for an hour or so, but wouldn't go near the sea, I'm not sure why but he seemed a bit afraid of it. He gave me a shell, which I pocketed as a momento for Rockall, and we enjoyed the sunshine and the sound of the lapping waves. Eventually we had to go, as I had forgotten to bring my watch with me. Apart from being important, this was also annoying as I had spent the last month getting used to wearing a watch again as I hadn't worn one for the past year or so. This was because I had realised that whenever we were on holiday or at the weekend, I would take my watch off and not look at. This seemed to make my free time last longer and certainly reduced the stress associated with time keeping which I had to do to get to appointments at work. So, I had decided to stop wearing it all together, which seemed to have a positive effect on me mentally. Therefore, I had to get used to wearing a watch again.

I found a watch in the first shop in Tarbert we went to, and then I popped along to the new Kilda Cruises' office to check in with Angus' wife and to see if there was any change to the proposed departure, which there was not. We headed back to Lickisto and spent the rest of the evening adventuring with Freddie down the campsite's many vegetated paths and over its wooden bridges, before settling in for the night. Needless to say, in a light canvas tent with windows and a sky light, at that time of year, Freddie didn't settle until late and we got a second poor night's sleep in a row.

The next day (Wednesday) we breakfasted and headed down to meet up with Angus at Orca 3, in Leverburgh, first stopping at the Am Bothan bunkhouse, where we met up with Ruari and unloaded all Pam's, Freddie's and my shore kit into their room before driving down to the pier. There Angus and the crew were part way through fuelling the boat and filling the extra fuel drums lashed on her decks for the journey out to Rockall. Once that was complete, the boat was moved to below the pier crane and the lads helped me get the RockPod out of the back of the van and over to the crane, whereupon it was hoisted onto the rear deck of Orca 3, as practiced, and lashed down tight.

Reproduced with permission Kilda Cruises

There followed a chain of people passing my kit barrels, water containers, Pelicase containing the satellite communications kit, and an 'overnight' bag which held my dry suit and buoyancy aid for the landing ahead. Before long (around 1300) it was time to depart and I hugged and kissed Pam and Freddie goodbye and waved until I could no longer make them out on the pier. Pam was quite upset; Freddie was just excited that I was on a boat with the RockPod and heading to Rockall!

The cruise out to the rock took about fifteen hours and was fairly uneventful. I felt queasy, despite the drugs I was taking and wrist bands I wore, which surprised me as on the two previous trips out to Rockall the conditions were much rougher and I had no symptoms at all. Later, Pete, one of the experienced crew, said he'd also felt a tad ill, which suggests that there must have been something peculiar about the sea state that day.

Day 1 - 5th June

I slept off and on for about twelve of the fifteen hours out to Rockall and when I finally got up it was just breaking dawn and Rockall was visible on the horizon. Both the Anguses, or the 'Angii' as they were sometimes known, thought that conditions looked good and before long the crew were roused and I was suiting up.

The tenders were both put over the side using the boat's crane, and I jumped into the second before it left Orca 3. There followed a bit of swapping of crew until Angus was happy that the set up was right and we headed over the one hundred or so metres of sea to Rockall. The RIB I was on took a circuit of the rock to check the landing spot and have a look at a possible northern landing point which I had read about, which also look feasible. We decided to head for the 'traditional' Western spot and Angus powered the tender up to the cliff.

I landed around 0630 on 5th June 2014. This year conditions were so good that I could almost step out of the tender onto the rock, but not quite; a little leap and then a scramble up the fissure that climbs diagonally up the western face and marks the start of the route to the summit. I heard Ruari land behind me, but was keen to get to a safe point above the surf and so pushed on around the corner, over a small overhang, and up onto the more reasonable northern slope. At this point Angus shouted to me to go back for Ruari who did not know the route, and just as I dropped a couple of feet, he appeared round the corner and I was able to point out where he should climb up to my position. We both then continued together onto the summit ridge, where I descended to Hall's Ledge and Ruari went up onto the platform at the top.

I then quickly set about getting out my light yellow line which I threw down to Angus in the tender in order that we could bring up the two dry bags containing the heavier, longer ropes, pulleys and the Portable Winch which I would use to bring the RockPod up the vertical East face. Having rigged the ropes, as close to the set up I'd practiced with Fraser and Stevie at EICA Ratho as was possible on Hall's Ledge, I unpacked the winch to see a small pool of oil in the bottom of the case. I had last started the winch in Leverburgh before we left and all was well, but now the winch wouldn't start. Ruari thought that being bounced around on the boat and again on its side during the haul up had caused oil to leak into the cylinder. We contacted the boat and they sent up some tools in a dry bag. Ruari managed to remove the spark plug and expel the oil after about twenty minutes work. Once the oil was cleared, the winch started first time. Angus then hauled the two winch ropes, a black static safety line and a white doubled rope with a pulley attached, down to the tender, which upon being informed that the winch was working, had returned to Orca 3 to collect the RockPod.

Reproduced with permission Kilda Cruises

There followed a bit of shouting between me and Angus to make sure that the ropes were attached to the RockPod in the correct positions and that the right, black one, was above the white one. Angus confirmed that the ropes were attached and I visually checked from my position before returning to the haul rig to double check that was set, and then restart the winch. As expected, once the winch was started we couldn't hear the VHF and there was obviously something happening below. I stopped hauling and went to see, but Angus shouted that all was ok and we pushed on. It turned out that the RockPod had partially flipped during the transition from the sea to the rock face, but that the guys on the tender had managed to right it quickly without too much fuss, as I had hoped.

Reproduced with permission Kilda Cruises

The now well-practiced process of winching the RockPod up the side of Rockall continued smoothly and without a hitch. Fraser and Stevie would have been proud. The edge transition, which had always proved to be difficult in practice at Ratho, went very smoothly in reality, with the only interference needed being to make sure that the pulley didn't get caught on the anti-friction mat hanging over the edge, and Ruari and myself having to lift the front edge of the base of the RockPod over one of the old fixings Greenpeace had drilled into the rock.

Angus then sent Peter, one of the crew, up the rock in order to help Ruari and me man-haul the remainder of my kit, in the blue Smiths of Dean drums, and my water jerry cans up the vertical face onto Hall's Ledge. This was hard physical work, but with three of us the ten barrels and seven water containers came up quickly, followed by the wind turbine mast and the case containing the communications kit (once I had asked Angus to go back to the Orca 3 to get it!). Ruari had been lashing the drums down as he went, so everything was quickly, albeit temporarily, secure on a flat area at the East end of Hall's Ledge which Ruari decided would be my patio, and once all that was done, Alasdair, another crew member, joined us as the landing conditions were so good. He had actually swum ashore to the hypothesised northern landing point and found it an easy enough landing spot, with decent climbing and no overhang.

Reproduced with permission Kilda Cruises

At this point I felt it was safe enough for me to set off my SPOT Messenger which had a pre-programmed message going to family, friends and my Press Officer Iain Maciver saying that both I and the RockPod were safe and secure on Hall's Ledge. The news was out! Alasdair was up with the rest of us on Hall's Ledge for ten to fifteen minutes before they decided to leave and head back down to the boat, which they did with the aid of a rope down the northern side of the rock. They left me about 0900 and appeared in the tender around 0915, so I estimate that I was left alone on the rock at 0910 on 5th June 2014.

It was a hot (23°c in the RockPod) and still day and I needed to wear a sun hat and glasses for the rest of the afternoon, which I spent, once Orca 3 had left, lashing down the RockPod with ratchet straps to the stainless steel fixings that Greenpeace had left in situ, and organising my kit drums so they were all secure behind the RockPod and between the ratchet straps. They were also strapped down to the pod and the fixings using a combination of ropes and the purple strops that had formed part of the hauling mechanism. Once the safety essentials were finished, I set about bringing food, clothing, and electronics into the RockPod while I had dry weather.

By the end of the day, I was feeling a bit down and homesick, even though I had been privileged to watch a minke whale off the eastern side of the rock for five minutes. Being so suddenly on my own in the middle of nowhere after two days before being on what was to all appearances a lovely family holiday in the Outer Hebrides, was a shock to the system. The wonders of modern satellite telecommunications meant that I was able to call my wife and having briefly spoken to her and my son, I felt much happier. It was then time to eat and sleep as I was fairly knackered after an early start and a physically demanding day.

Day 2 – 6th June

After ten hours of good sleep, I awoke to foggy conditions which was a stark contrast to yesterday when there was not a cloud in the sky. I couldn't see the horizon, and it was circa 23°c in the RockPod! It was drizzling too, and being fairly groggy after a long, much needed sleep I slowly went about making breakfast and a hot drink using the LP Gas and stove so kindly provided by Calor. I read some of 'Winchman' by Chris Murray QGM, which I had started the night before, while I waited for the weather to clear, which it did in the late morning. I also had the opportunity to test the black latrine bucket for the first time - a loo with a view!

As the afternoon was warmer and clearer I decided to get on with some important jobs: security of the RockPod and security of a power supply, without which I would not be able to communicate readily with my family nor send the now expected Tweets and Blogs to update the expedition's followers as to my state of mind and health.

The Greenpeace fixings looked and felt sound, but are pretty old having been placed some seventeen years ago, in 1997, so I added four more. I placed one almost at each corner of the RockPod, to which, once I am sure that the resin has set, I will secure two three-tonne ratchet straps over the top of the RockPod deck, running in moulded grooves in the shell which were designed to hold the full water bowser, weighting 2.5 tonnes, down to its trailer.

The next job, while I was in drilling mode and had resin to hand, was to go up on top of Rockall and recce a spot for my Ampair wind turbine. I had to take a number of issues into account: one, the blades would need to be free of any obstructions and have good exposure to the wind (not a problem on top of Rockall); two, birds were regularly using the old light housing for shelter and I did not want to disturb or restrict them more than I absolutely had to; three, I had to be able to get up to the summit safely, without being hit by the blades, in order to stop the turbine when or if I had to and also so that I could carry out the survey work that I intended to do later in the expedition. Having finally decided that the best place was the most obvious, right in the middle of the summit plateau, I went about fixing the base plate for the turbine mast. The holes for the base plate fixings were quite easily drilled with the same drill I had used earlier for the security fixings, a Bosch GBH 36 VF-LI, kindly leant to me by Webster Power Products. I then resin fixed the base plate to the rock and left it to dry overnight.

My final task for today was to go through my kit drums in a bit more detail and fish out more kit, equipment, food and dry clothes that I will need over the next few days. As you can imagine, the already tight internal space of the RockPod is now fairly full, although I can still stretch out to sleep, albeit in a space only the width of my body, which served to remind me yet again how glad I am that I'm not too tall! The other good thing about the pod being full is that there is less air space to heat with my body heat alone, although I'm sure that the seven water carriers will be acting as some sort of heat sink and regulating the internal temperature somewhat.

Day 3 – 7th June

Today it's rained most of the day; visibility was low and the winds fairly high. I was awoken by the gannets fighting for space on top of the rock and one unceremoniously flopped, with a loud thump, onto the deck of the RockPod and regurgitated a large pellet of fish! The gannet flew off, uninjured, leaving me the pellet to stare at, right at my eye line from the main pod hatch for the rest of the morning. Shortly afterwards, I was standing in the pod looking out at the sea and admiring the view, when out of nowhere I was hit squarely in the face and chest with bird poop. It was bound to happen at some point in the trip, on such a small speck of rock whose main inhabitants are birds; I just wasn't expecting it so soon. Anyway, after cleaning myself off, I decided that the old tradition of it being a good omen must be true and thanked the kind bird for his present.

Apart from that, I've had a fairly quiet morning due to the wind and rain, but during breaks in the weather managed to build the head of my Ampair wind turbine, which was a key task in order for me to start generating power. Wisely I had thought to build and test the turbine before I left home and I'm very glad I did. The turbine is very well engineered with fine tolerances in how the components fit together, which you would hope and expect. The problem for me, out here on my own, is that this makes it quite fiddly to put together. For example, the turbine blades bolt onto the rotating head between two metal plates, which squeeze together under pressure from the bolts to hold the blades in place. These bolts are a special shape with a square section under the domed bolt head before the threaded section, which fits into a socket in the outside plate.

In practice getting this square section into the socket required almost perfect alignment, requiring me to push, twist and pull the bolt into the right place before it would fit. In addition, the holes through the blades for the bolts were so tight a fit that the bolts originally had to be screwed through the blade holes. This would be too difficult on Rockall, and so after a test build at home I had drilled the blade holes out to make them perhaps half a millimetre wider which meant I could then push the bolts straight through. Something I was very glad I'd done when assembling the turbine today.

Once the wind turbine head was complete, which took me over an hour as I really didn't want to be dropping any of the nuts, bolts nor washers, even though I did have some spares, I turned to my small weather station that I've also brought with me. Part of the reason for bringing this was for my own interest and entertainment while on the rock. It has a wireless base station which I can keep inside the pod, and so I will know a rough forecast, from barometric pressure trends, wind direction and speed, and internal and external temperatures. All very useful stuff, although I could obviously guestimate most of this information by sticking my head out of the top hatch! It is, however, also my intention to leave the weather station in place when I leave Rockall, with the base unit sealed in a waterproof box inside the redundant light housing. Although there is no way the station will survive the winter, there is enough battery life in both parts for a year's worth of data collection, and it is my hope that the base unit will either stay inside the housing, weighted down as it will be by the three large batteries that have been left in there, or would be washed out and float off somewhere to be found and returned to me along with the data. I not sure how interested the Met Office will be in a period of 'live' data from Rockall, but if nothing else it is something else to do to pass the time.

My reason for building the weather station at this point is that I had decided that it also needs to be on top of Rockall to get the most exposure and hence the best readings, but I don't want it to be in the way when I have to go up to the summit it order to check the turbine or carry out my survey. That means that the logical place for it is out on the end of the summit platform, beyond the light housing, a place I don't want to venture too often as it is very exposed, with the vertical face below. If I built the station now, it means that as soon as I have its base fixing in place, the unit can start operating, can be forgotten about and be out of the way while I am setting up the guy lines for the turbine mast.

I had decided not to do any more work on the turbine mast today as it was just too wet and windy to be safe on top, even though I was tethered when I was up there. In addition, I've already found that when the weather is dry and warm or windy the summit is much dryer and so a safer place to be than when its wet or has been raining, when the guano becomes as slippery as soap. I am secretly hopeful that there will be some decent breaks in the weather tomorrow, so that I can complete the next big project of sorting out the guy wires for the turbine mast, mounting the head and getting the turbine up and running, and then recharging my twelve volt battery inside the RockPod.

Day 4 – 8th June

Today was a fine day and thankfully that meant that I could get on with the vital job of installing the wind turbine. Up to this point I have only been gingerly recharging essential kit in order to maintain communications, but with wind power comes the luxury of recharging iPods and cameras.

The first job was to secure the guy wires for the turbine mast. The base seemed to have set well enough with the resined in bolts, so I went about extending the four guy wires out to see where they would lie naturally. The southernmost dropped over the edge of the summit onto the face above Hall's Ledge, and looked as if it might just fasten onto one of two existing fixings in that area. The northern one went over the edge down the face on that side, which was not great news as there are few bolts in this area, which may mean that I have to put in a new one specifically to make it safe to descend the face in order to attach the guy wire. The easterly one will have to run over the top of the old light housing, but will then reach the rock on the summit beyond, and the westerly will also need a new tether point, but on the route I take up to the summit, and so should be fairly easy to install.

On each of the guy wires I have previously attached a screw tensioner to allow me to tighten up the lines once in place. It quickly became obvious that the line I'd hoped would attach to the existing fixings on the south face will need a new bolt as they are just too high. In addition, I played around with the northern line, removing the tensioner and wrapping the line around the fixings on the summit to see if I could achieve the required angle and tension, but not to a satisfactory level. However, in the process of this experiment, I did uncover another of Greenpeace's old ring bolts on the north side of the summit plateau, which had been hidden under a pile of seaweed. This is in the perfect place to allow me to descend the north face safely enough to install the required new fixing; problem solved. A final recce around the back of the light housing confirmed that the wire in that area will reach nicely and there was even an old bolt sticking out of the top of the housing which will help guide the wire as it changed angle across the top of the housing and prevent it slipping out of line.

Tactics decided, I began the to-ing and fro-ing required to shuttle tools and the Raumer hanging plates that will be the guy wire tethers up onto the summit. This is one of the issues with working alone in such an exposed location; you cannot afford to drop anything, and because it's a scramble to the summit, you cannot have too much in your hands. The drill was tethered to my climbing harness, drill bit pre-fitted before the ascent, a hammer for the Raumer plates in one of my harness gear loops, and the plates in a zipped pocket. I started with the southern wire, as I could work on that from below, just above Hall's Ledge, with a reasonably stable standing point. The plates were fixed by drilling a hole in the rock, inserting an expanding bolt, to which the plate is moulded, and then hammering home the bolt to force the section within the hole to expand and grip. All in all a quick and easy process, and one recommended to me by the climber Andy Cave.

Next came the fiddly bit: each of the rigging screw tensioners has a loose bolt in the base held in place with a metal ring, similar to a key ring. This ring had to be removed to allow the bolt to slide back for the tensioner to go over the fixing plate. The bolt is then replaced and the ring reinserted to lock the bolt in place. This would be tricky enough at a dining table, but at a funny angle in the middle of nowhere, with a less than perfect stance, it required a lot of concentration and patience in order not to drop the bolt or ring. Fortunately, some clever soul had designed the ring so the tip of the loop end was bent in such a way that it caught into the hole in the bolt, which made inserting it much easier.

The southern wire in place, I moved onto the exposed northern one, partly to get it done and out of the way, and partly because the turbine mast could hinge on its base plate east-west, which it would need to in order to allow me to get the turbine head on and thread the electric cable down through the mast. I could do this with both the north and south wires in place, so I thought it best to get them fixed and the mast at least partially supported. Clambering up onto the summit with the large Bosch drill from Websters was not easy, but I clipped into the newly revealed anchor and descended down the few metres to where the end of the northern wire lay. Making sure this was in line with the mast, I again drilled a hole and fixed the plate, attaching the tensioner without too much fuss. I was then able to turn the tensioner and achieve a reasonable level of support for the vertical mast on this north-south axis.

Next was the easterly mounting, beyond the light housing and right on the edge of the vertical east face of Rockall. As I was going out to this point, and didn't want to have to very often, I'd also previously brought up the base plate for the weather station so that I could drill the holes to fix that too. Holes drilled, I screwed the weather station base down and hammered the Raumer plate home. It's probably worth mentioning that the weather station I fixed the base with normal rawl-plug type fixings and screws. The reason I used these rather than resin fixing the plate was that I was certain that the station would be destroyed in the winter storms if not before, and hoped the base might be taken away too so as not to leave too much un-necessary metal work on the rock.

The westerly plate went in just as easily as the others, and before descending to the RockPod with the drill and tools, I went about evening up the guy wires as much as possible, without them being fully tensioned, so that the turbine mast was in the right position for accepting the head once I had brought that up. Earlier, I had also used one of the guy wires to pull a length of paracord down through the mast, which I would subsequently use to pull the electric cable through.

The next job was to get the turbine head up the summit. I mentioned previously that, due to the poor weather, I had built it in stages the day before. I had also attached a pair of short chains to two fixings on the southern edge of the summit; using these, I now lifted up and clipped the turbine head to one. This meant that the head was already half way up the face of the rock above Hall's Ledge, and I just had to go up to the top and pull it the rest of the way up. Both the lifting and the pulling were made harder as the turbine had its six blades and tail on, which made it quite unwieldy, plus I obviously didn't want to damage the resin blades or bend the tail, so pulling it to the top with the chain was a slow business with the various parts catching on every rock feature as it came up. Eventually it was up and I then had to find space for it on the summit, while I sorted out the guy wires and lent the mast down. Having tried to pull the wire through the mast with it at around forty five degrees, I realised that the gap where it would exit at the base of the mast was just too small to accommodate the wire moving through the ninety degree bend required for it to come out and so I had to lie the mast completely flat, which necessitated completely disconnecting the easterly tensioner, in the exposed position, with the fiddly connectors!

With the wire through, the head slipped easily onto the mast, which I then pushed to the vertical. I had previously tied off the blades so that they would not start spinning at this stage, first of all to protect me and secondly because the wires would become live as soon as the blades started turning. For some reason, holes for bolts never line up first time, so I had to lift and twist the head until I could get the restraining bolt into the neck to finally secure the head to the mast. It was then just a matter of reconnecting the tensioner I had disconnected and tensioning up all the guy wires so that they were tight and holding the mast and head as near vertical as I could get them.

Electrics came next, and I had pre-mounted the charge controller inside the RockPod before departure. The battery was also now in the pod having been hauled up in by far the heaviest blue drum of all. Working backwards, I first connected the battery to the charge controller, which was as simple as screwing two O rings to the battery terminals. The main power cable from the controller exited the pod through a rubber grommet in the top deck, which was marine grade and sealed. Then I just had to connect the wire from the controller to the wire from the turbine using a basic junction box within an IP55 rated waterproof outdoor housing.

The only issue I had was that the junction box needed a flat head screwdriver and I only seemed to have brought Phillips with me. I was sure that I had packed a flat head, but couldn't find it on my barrel contents lists, and so started hunting around for a suitable alternative, such as a knife tip or similar, when I realised that I had been too clever for my own good and that the required screwdriver was in a bag with all my electrical spares! Having double and triple checked the wiring and connections, I released the turbine and blades and it turned to face the wind and started spinning. A hopeful clamber back down to the pod revealed the satisfying green glow of the charging light on the controller, and I was in business. The final task was to tidy the wiring, gaffa taping it to the wall of the pod internally and plasti-tying it down externally at various points to the pod and the rock fixings so that it didn't blow about in the wind or get snagged.

Tools away, and having spent most of the day on this one task, I sat and relaxed, admiring the new white sentinel quietly spinning away on the summit of Rockall, providing me with lovely free electricity with which to charge my cameras, laptop, satellite communications equipment, and phones.

Day 5 – 9th June

I awoke this morning about 0830, which seems to be becoming the norm as I settle into this slower pace of life. Eventually, I cajoled myself up and opened the hatch to find that the Windguru forecast was thankfully correct, medium winds (21kph), hazy sky and far reaching views – a fine day. Happily, too, the wind turbine had survived its first night on top of Rockall without any of the resident bird life flying into it at full speed. Hopefully, after a day or so, they'll be aware of its presence and there will be no further risk. There is the added benefit that most of the bird life now seems to have moved to the other face of Rockall, or to ledge below and beside me, which will also hopefully mean no more incidents of heavy gannets plummeting onto the deck of the RockPod after a fight for space on the summit! The birds too seem to be enjoying the weather, with the guillemots getting frisky and mating all over the place and the kittiwakes were also at it yesterday.

A gannet, which I have christened 'Spud', has appeared in the old light housing on top of the rock. Yesterday he looked very dirty and a bit weak. I suspect if he wants to get out he would take off into the wind. However, as one of the guy lines for the wind turbine now runs across the top of the housing on the southern side (the side where the wind is coming from today and was also yesterday), although it only restricts about a quarter or less of the opening, he is perhaps unable to get out. I was hoping to avoid going back up there too much as the light housing is by far the dirtiest and smelliest spot on the rock, full of bird faeces, dead birds and rotting eggs, and when the birds fly out of it they tend to spray you with the festering liquid. I'll keep an eye on him from down here, and will check on him from a distance later on today or tomorrow, if he's still there. I may have to step in and pull him out, which I'd prefer not to do, as it will not just be smelly and messy, but also potentially dangerous as the gannet's beak is long, sharp and pointed for spearing fish!

There was also a strange but interesting phenomenon this morning. It's obviously due to the particular wind direction, which is currently south easterly, but one of the ratchet straps at the eastern end of the RockPod started to periodically vibrate and buzz with a loud humming noise, which was a bit of a surprise to begin with, but has now become annoying!

Now having the luxury of wind generated power, I spent most of this morning recharging key pieces of electronics such as my satellite phones and laptop, before attempting to get into the slower pace of 'Rockall Time' now that I do not have the urgent jobs of safety, security, and power to sort as quickly as possible. After lunch, and still with loose bowels, I thought of a couple more jobs to do to keep me busy for the afternoon. The first of these was to put the rubbish out, which sounds simple enough, but bearing in mind I was living in a confined space, cleanliness is key, so I have set Barrel 10 up as my rubbish bin and all the wrappings from the previous few days' food have gone in there sealed away from everything else. Then I had to manually tip out the latrine bucket; previously I had just been tipping it down 'Gardyloo Gully', but the wind was blowing straight at me today, so I thought better of that. Next was a bit of maintenance: during the rain the other day a leak appeared around the hinge of the main entrance hatch to the RockPod. I thought I had identified the source and that along with the grommet where the newly installed electric cable entered the pod, but where the rubber seal did not quite close properly, I sealed with marine grade silicone that I had brought for just such a purpose.

Having completed those jobs, I decided to explore a little further while it was warm and dry and so less slippery. I went down onto The Patio and had a look back at Hall's Ledge, as you get a good perspective from there, and can also look down over the edge. I spotted a couple of seals playing in the surf, and to my surprise a pigeon appeared! I'm guessing that it is a racing pigeon as it had two rings on its legs, a red one on the right and a green one on the left. Although it seemed perfectly happy, and even walked to within a metre of me, I was unable to read any markings so cannot shed any more light on it for now. Anyway, I left him to it and walked up The Ramp to the leeward side of the summit to take in the view. Eventually, I returned to the summit and was pleased to see that Spud the gannet was no longer in the light housing, so hopefully he has made a clean (literally) escape and is well. Taking the opportunity, while up there, I looked around for a good spot for the survey markers I hope to install later in the trip and found a flat spot which I was able to clear of debris and brush down in preparation. I also brushed off the only plaque on the summit which is a facsimile of one on the plaque wall at the end of Hall's Ledge. I have no idea, and have not been able to find out, why there are two copies of the same plaque in different locations on Rockall, and can only guess that one was thought lost and so 'replaced' at some point in the past.

Day 6 – 10th June

I saw my first solitary puffin today. The most common animals out here are birds and really that is all there is apart from two or three seals that appear at the base of the rock every now and again, and a minke whale which reappeared today after I saw it briefly on day one just after the boat left.

The most common birds here are gannets and guillemots, although there are also kittiwakes, fulmars, and a few razorbills. Yesterday's big surprise was that a pigeon turned up! Not a lovely fat woodpigeon but the Trafalgar Square type of rock dove. Normally I'm not a fan, but it was nice to sit and watch it pootle around the rock looking vainly for some scraps, the iridescent green and pink on its neck glimmering in the sun. It even flew round the other side of the rock on some hopeless quest for more land, but soon returned and came very close so that I could see it had two leg rings, red on the right, with the number 496, and green on the left. I'm assuming it's a lost racing pigeon. It was still here this morning, and I fed it a bit of biscuit brown, but I couldn't read any of the markings on the green band to pass on to a pensive owner.

I have a bird identification chart with me as I'm not really a twitcher, but I have three mystery birds already. One was small, brown and has a long thin beak. There seems to be two types, one with a white belly and one without. Male and female perhaps? The second is about the size of a kittiwake, but has a grey band across the back of its neck, a black band across the tip of its tail, and patchy grey wings[20]. The third is a larger bird which is mostly dark brown/black in colour, I don't think it's a skua, with a white band across the back of its neck and a long thin tail feather trailing behind a bit like a bird of paradise[21].

In other news, the Ampair wind turbine is holding up to some pretty strong winds, which hopefully means I've put it up well enough, and is silently spinning away lighting the lovely green charging light on my battery charge controller. Not only does this mean that I don't have to be quite so frugal with my power usage (Italian lessons may start soon!) but it also means that I can pretty much guarantee that I'll have enough power to transmit live to television in the next few days, which will be a first. I unfortunately missed a slot on BBC Breakfast on Sunday morning due to low thick cloud and high winds meaning that we could not do the test call, but the forecast is fair for the rest of the week, so I'm hopeful I'll be able to do something.

Aside from that, the transition to 'Rockall Time' is going well. I'm definitely slowing down and fitting tasks to the time I have rather than rushing to get stuff done as I would at home, or had to in the first few days here. At home or work, and almost without realising it, we all conduct activities concurrently. You may not know you're doing it, but it's innate and we use it to achieve more in a given time. For example, and this is relevant to Rockall, you may have a cup of tea while reading a newspaper or filling in a form, or even while on the phone at work. That's because you have a lot to do and a set time in which to achieve it. That, with the exception of the first few days

---

[20] I later identified this as a juvenile kittiwake.
[21] I identified this as a long-tailed skua on my return home.

when there were urgent tasks to complete like securely tying down the RockPod and setting up the wind turbine, does not apply on Rockall. With a thermal insulated mug, I can take half an hour just to sit and enjoy drinking a cup of tea, while admittedly concurrently watching the birds fly about, fishing boats pass by, or thinking about what I might do next. Only then would I go about typing up my diary, or doing personal admin, or cleaning the RockPod floor.

I'm also getting a lot of, if fitful, sleep at night which obviously eats into the hours. Health wise, I'm also (touch wood) not too bad either. I picked up a calf strain in the first couple of days which seems to be slowly getting better, and a cut on my finger, which I got while landing and had, unsurprisingly, become infected has also cleared up and appears to be healing well thanks to a combination of the medical kit provide by Dr Mike Boyle and the waterproof Showa 377 work gloves I was asked to test out here, protecting it from the guano while I was out and about the past few days.

I wrote most of the above this morning, and may have spoken too soon about security of power. Just after lunch the sky cleared and the wind dropped to nothing, which is lovely to see, but means no power generation. It's been the same all afternoon, and I've had to retreat to the RockPod for some shade after an afternoon of collecting water samples for St. Andrews University, and a few flies for the Hunterian Museum. The pigeon's still here and it definitely has a code on the green band, although I may have to catch it in order to read it.

I'm also very excited as tomorrow is clean underpants day. I may have a small party!

Day 7 – 11th June

Every time I look up from my main hatch in the RockPod and see the wind turbine spinning it gives me a great sense of achievement in having managed to erect it out here on my own, but also in that it goes some way towards me being in 'control' of my environment. Additionally, it tells me which way the wind is blowing, which is important when having a pee, and also approximately how strong it is, even before I pop my head out for the first time each day.

It's strange how things, tastes, smells, etc. can remind you of places and times. One of my favourite quotes is from John Donne's 'Elegies', "I turn that scent like a memorial key". Last night, before bed, I had a mint flavoured hot chocolate. There were some remnants of it in the cup this morning, and not having enough water to do washing up, I've just been making my next hot drink in the same cup, residue and all, wiping down the rim periodically with a wet wipe. Anyway, this morning I had my first 'coffee' of the trip. I say 'coffee' as it was instant and I'm a bit of a coffee snob. However, with the added hint of chocolate and mint, the taste and smell reminded me of walking through Greenwich Market in London, looking at all the knick-knacks and wandering past the flavoured coffee stalls. It was nice to drift away, and I lay back and enjoyed the memory for a while.

Today was also my first 'clean underpants day'. Six and a bit days in and I was feeling the need for a change. Often expedition blogs, books or reports fail to talk about the small details, tending to focus on the larger logistical issues and the greater overall aim. Unless you've wild camped, been on an expedition of any size, or spent time in the military cadets or scouts, how are you supposed to fully understand the day to day life of an expedition without these details? So, save it to say that I needed a change, and it was a great relief that after daily ablutions, I could discard the old pair, have a proper wipe down of the nether regions with some wet wipes and slip into a lovely clean pair of pants, which, I have to admit, I did smell for quite a long time before putting on, just to remind myself what clean smells like. It's good and I can tell you that it feels pretty good too; small mercies. I even composed a brief 'clean underpants' song off the cuff, which I proceeded to sing, very untunefully, at the top of my voice as no-one can hear me out here!

In addition to it being clean underpants day, it was also clean sock day. In the process of putting said socks on this morning, I discovered one of my wife's long blonde hairs in one of the socks, which must have got caught in there during a wash. It was oddly nice to think of having part of her with me here, strange what's good for morale, and so I carefully taped it with some gaffa tape to the ceiling of the RockPod as a keepsake of her. I suppose in the past, I would have put it in a locket or some male equivalent, but I didn't have one, so gaffa tape would have to do.

I decide after lunch to carry out a few minor jobs. These included going through some of the kit drums in a bit more detail to find another couple of books, a harmonica, and some more tools I might need in the coming days. Those tasks duly completed, I sat for a while on the patio and noticed that the wind turbine blades seemed to be out of line when spinning. I had also seen a few days before that at certain speeds the mast wobbled above the guy wire tethering point. This had surprised me, because as previously mentioned, the turbine is so well made. The day was dry and wind not too high so I decided to investigate. The turbine is easily stopped, assuming you can grab the tail vane without being hit by the blade, by turning it out of the wind. I checked each of the six blades in turn and could see nothing obviously wrong until I looked side on and spun them. One of the blade tips was further forward that the rest. I quickly realised that this was because it was on back to front, and although I had checked that the declination of each blade was correct as I was building the head the other day, I obviously didn't notice that one was turned 180 degrees in its mount.

This meant I had to go back down to the pod to collect the tools I would need as well as a length of paracord in order to tie off the rotor head while I was working on it, so that it didn't take my arm off! Climbing back to the top, and tying off the rotor, it was simply a matter of unbolting the tight fitting bolts, not losing the nuts and washers down the side of Rockall, turning the blade and tightening everything back up again. I'm very pleased to say that the turbine is now spinning at a high RPM, nothing looks out of line, and there is no 'wobble'. I shall continue to monitor it over the next few days in varying wind speeds, but hopefully that has done the trick. I'm glad I noticed!

Towards the end of the day I decided that it was about time I put up my 'Help for Heroes' banner. I had put the same banner up on Rockall when I landed briefly in 2012, and thought it would be good to erect it again as I will see it every time I get out of the RockPod and it will remind me why I am sat here in the middle of nowhere. It's very easily put up, as it has eight holes around the edge, to which I secured ten bungee cords, which hooked onto the various rock fixings on the back wall leading up to the summit. It looked great in the sun and I hope it'll withstand the worst of the winds so that I won't have to take it down before I leave.

Day 8 – 12th June

I woke up to high winds (25mph/40kph) and rain, not a great start, and this continued for the whole morning. It was the sort of weather where at home you would sit under a duvet and watch movies, and I didn't fancy doing very much, so I just pondered life, caught up on my diary, and watched the birds dancing in the wind above my main hatch as I lay on my back in the pod. I did spot an Arctic Tern, which I hope will be a first, and there were the usual gulls, guillemots and kittiwakes.

The pigeon was still here this morning too, sheltering from the wind behind the RockPod, and with its feathers puffed up to keep it warm. We've progressed to hand feeding the odd crumb now, and if I'm sat in the pod with my head out, it'll come right up and look to try and get in too, being only a couple of inches from my face. Interestingly, I've noticed that there have been hardly any gannets around for the past few days; however, just as they left, a crowd of greater black-backed gulls have appeared. I'm not sure what that indicates, but is does make for some variety, especially as I'm not a huge fan of the gannets, their smell and their noise.

In the high winds today, the turbine has been spinning very fast and not a sniff of a wobble nor anything out of line, so I am very glad I dealt with the incorrectly fitted blade yesterday when I had the time. The wind has meant, though, that I've gone from power famine to feast. Having been wary about what I used and charged to begin with, before the turbine was up and on the day that I had no wind at all, today the charge controller kicked into 'dump' mode which essentially means that the main lead acid battery is fully charged and that the power being generated is being dumped as heat. This is not a major issue, although I feel that it can't be a great thing for the system to be generating heat for too long, so I recharged my VHF and iPod, and have been running the laptop off the battery all afternoon. The wind is still high, so I suspect it might 'dump' again overnight.

Day 9 – 13th June

I was up early today at 0600, as I had my alarm set in order to check emails and see if BBC Breakfast had sent me a time that they wanted to interview me live on TV. Very annoyingly they hadn't, which didn't surprise me as their team seem to be unable to grasp the fact that I'm not online in normal business hours, nor that I have a limited power supply. Grumbling, I went back to bed and was pleased to reawaken at almost 0930! The usual morning routine of setting off my SPOT messenger, followed by ablutions and breakfast followed.

Yesterday I had decided that today I would definitely set up and start my Leica GNSS satellite survey kit, with which I hope to pin point the exact height and position on Rockall. From this data I should be able to extrapolate the actual height of Hall's Ledge, which up to now has been a best guess, and as I will leave a fixed survey marker, in the future further readings can be taken to measure any movement in position or height of the rock.

I was disappointed not to see the grey pigeon all morning, and had assumed that a new brown interloper had scared it off (or perhaps he had rested enough and was on its way home). Either way it got me to thinking why they might still be here. They can't be hungry as they're not eating the crumbs I've left out, nor thirsty as there's plenty of fresh rainwater caught in my drum lids for them. After a couple of days, you would have thought they would be well enough rested to move on too. My hypothesis is that the magnetic anomaly around Rockall has them confused. Perhaps they landed for a rest and now do not know which way to fly on. I've seen both pigeons fly a long way away from the rock, only to return, and there have been strong both easterly and westerly winds, if they were waiting for either of those. Who knows?

The hole for the survey marker was again easily drilled in the summit platform. I had been advised by Leica to place it somewhere obvious and easily found for any future survey, and they had even gone so far as to suggest within the old light housing. The problem with this was twofold: the housing has a solid base, is not open to the rock; and secondly, the light might at some point be reinstated which would cover the survey marker. As it happened there was one section between the grooves left by the drill used to place the explosives to remove the top of Rockall that was flatter and smoother than the other sections. It won't be hard to find again as the top is not that large, and the marker has a yellow plastic collar around it in order to make it easy to find.

The marker is basically an expanding socket which is hammered into the hole, and then a threaded lug is screwed into that, onto which one can screw any standard sized surveying mount. In this case it was two 40cm lengths of carbon fibre pole to which the GNSS satellite aerial was screwed, forming a kind of elongated mushroom. A wire ran from the aerial to the recording box, which I just had to switch on and it automatically located the satellites and started recording. I placed the box within the light housing for protection, and left it for what I hoped would be around twenty four hours of data gathering. The whole set up took around half an hour, and I will repeat it towards the end of the expedition in order to obtain comparable data, which I am told will enable a more accurate position to be fixed as the satellites will be in different places. I do have a second survey marker, which I am undecided whether to use. I had thought that I might use it to accurately measure the height of Hall's Ledge or alternatively place a second marker on the summit in order to ascertain the orientation of the rock, but I will decide later.

In the early afternoon the wind dropped, the turbine stopped again and it became quite hot. At these times the coolest spot is within the RockPod, out of the direct sun, with the hatches ajar to allow a slight breeze through. I had been asked to Skype Inmarsat in order to discuss a couple of minor technical issues, which it turns out might also be as a result of the magnetic anomaly around Rockall, and their PR strategy for promoting the expedition and their support of it. During that call the sun was so hot that I was forced to wear a hat as I sat in the pod with head sticking out of the top hatch.

It has been really great to have Inmarsat on board, with the introduction made by Graham Hart-Ives, now at Wireless Innovation, whom I first spoke to a couple of years ago when planning the expedition. He then worked for a much larger satellite communications company; they didn't continue their support of Rockall Solo this year, but thankfully Graham did and that means that, via Inmarsat and a Cobham Explorer BGAN unit, people can read my blog and Tweets, and I can communicate with the outside world on a fairly regular basis, which is important, not just to tell the story and spread the word about the expedition in the hope that I will raise more funds for Help for Heroes, but also for my own sanity!

Today has also had the highest swell I've seen here so far, which was forecast and I expect it is a result of the high winds yesterday. It's difficult to tell the height from up on the ledge, but it was obviously higher, from the south, and with more breakers and higher splashes around the base of the rock. It was in fact forecast to be two to four metres. I believe that what little tide is out here must also have been low today as I got some very clear pictures of Hasselwood Rock, to the north, exposed clearly above the water as the swell passed by. I saw a seal out there, and assume it's one of those I've seen on numerous occasions at the base of Rockall, hunting for fish. In addition, I notice breakers far off to the east, just over three kilometres away, which I suspect is Helen's Reef, but not having a chart with me I will have to check that on my return[22].

---

[22] I confirmed on my return home, using The Royal Geographical Society's 1975 chart 'The Highest Part of the Rockall Bank', that it was indeed Helen's Reef that I could see.

Day 10 - 14th June

This morning I felt a pang of proper boredom for the first time!

The days are quietening down more now as I have fewer pre-planned big jobs to be getting on with, and if the weather allows, I'm generally taking the morning very slowly carrying out general admin, writing my blog and diary, and saving anything I have to do outside the pod for the afternoons. It can now take me up to an hour to have breakfast and finish my cup of tea or coffee. I wish I had the time to do that at home sometimes.

This morning I reached for a small book of knots that I brought out with me, and managed, I'm proud to say, to tie my first monkey's fist, a complex and ornate knot used to weigh down the end of a rope, which I've always fancied doing, but never seem to have the time. I'm fairly chuffed with it for a first go, but will try and perfect it. This small book, along with the knot 'bible', the 'Ashley Book of Knots', as recommended by the ocean rower Leven Brown, which I have on PDF, are amongst the things that I've brought with me to keep my mind active and stave off the boredom. Most of them, like the harmonica and Italian lessons, I'm going to try and leave until I absolutely have to resort to them. In the meantime, it's still nice to enjoy actually having the time to think, ponder and enjoy my ever changing surroundings, which I'm not sure I've had the time to do since I was a teenager.

In the afternoon, I took down the GNSS survey kit and backed up the data collected over the past twenty four hours or so, which I was not sure I would be able to do as planned, as it rained shortly after lunch, and as described before, the summit is not a nice place to be when it's wet. I'll repeat the whole process at least once, if not twice more while I'm here in order to get several datasets when the relevant satellites are in different positions. In this way, hopefully, I'll get the most accurate position and height for Rockall recorded. While out of the RockPod and looking for jobs to do, I also used a weighted rope, as the cliff on the East side of the rock was leeward of the wind, and took some rough measurements of the height of the summit plateau and the height of the lip at the top of the cliff just below Hall's Ledge, from the seaweed line. These were 17.5 metres and 14.2 metres respectively. Hall's Ledge is a little higher than the lip, and is generally supposed to be about 15 metres above sea level, so it will be interesting to see how my rough measurements match up to the satellite data.

In bird news, I had an arctic tern hovering over the rock the day before yesterday, which was pretty exciting, and in the past few days, most of the gannets have disappeared only to be replaced with greater black backed gulls. The general consensus seemed to be that my mystery birds from the other day were a juvenile kittiwake, a long tailed skua, and a red shank. There seemed to be some interest that the red shank was here, so perhaps that's a first sighting on Rockall?

Having thought that my friend the grey pigeon had left upon arrival of the new brown interloper, it would appear that it is still around and has finally started eating the crumbs I've left out for it on the deck of the RockPod. It's getting much more trusting too, even trying to come in the pod on a couple of occasions, and I've been able to stroke it, but am no closer to getting the rest of the numbers from its leg rings. The brown pigeon, however, has very clear markings on its rings, which is just as well as it is not so trusting. A light blue ring on the left leg reads '2635', and a green ring on its right leg reads 'GB13 B 33356'. I don't know if there's a central pigeon fanciers' database somewhere, but perhaps with the power of the internet I might be able to track down the owner and let him know where his bird(s) are[23].

I was also looking forward to visitors tomorrow, but more of that if it happens.

---

[23] A kind man called Dave Ferigan let me know that it was registered to a member of the Ballyholland Homing Pigeon Society, Newry, County Down, Northern Ireland.

Day 11 – 15th June

I awoke slightly earlier than normal today, which is not great news as that means more time to fill during the day. As it was, I managed to string breakfast and ablutions out a bit longer, despite the mysterious lack of food remaining in the current ration bag. I'm pretty sure a main meal has gone missing, but I've not been hungry, so it's not the end of the world. My food supply is basically thirty days military rations, with a couple of days extra, for sixty days. This might not sound enough, but when you consider that a day's ration pack averages around 4,500 calories, and the average man back home doing a normal day's work needs around 2,500 calories, the fact that I'm averaging around 2,250 calories a day when I'm not walking very far, doing anything very physical, nor having to really keep myself warm as I have good warm clothing and the RockPod is well insulated, then I should be fine. Despite this, I did treat myself in the run up to the expedition and put on a few pounds in order to give me something to lose if I had to.

The gannets have reappeared in numbers, so I think they must just have been away fishing, or perhaps they only use Rockall as a rest stop when the wind is higher, as it is today. I spent the morning reading an Historic Scotland research paper on a rural vernacular building (an interest of mine), and on the lookout for the 'Mary Slim' which was due to arrive today around midday on its speed attempt from Portland Bill around Rockall and back, crewed by Sebastian Courtauld and Richard Reddyhoff. I've not seen either pigeon today, but perhaps they are sheltering from the wind under the pod, which I've noticed them do, or on the leeward north side of the rock; the wind is south westerly today.

Once the afternoon came, I decided to move out onto the rock and carry out a few tasks. The first of which was to stop the wind turbine, as the wind speed was relatively high today, the charge controller had been dumping heat all morning, indicating that the main battery was fully charged, and I had run out of equipment to charge. I mentioned before that I did not think it wise to have the unit dumping for a prolonged period of time, in addition to the fact that the interior of the pod was warming up as a result of this and that it was a mild day. So, as I was not in urgent need of power, I thought it wise to stop the turbine for a couple of hours.

In thinking about kit to charge up, I remembered that there was a relatively full battery still on the drill, so I thought this would be a good opportunity to use some of that up, and then recharge them both, by cutting the recesses for the two commemorative plaques I brought with me. The first of these was a replica of a plaque removed from Rockall by John Coull, who landed in 1982, as it was apparently only stuck on with a thread of adhesive and was about to be lost to the sea. The plaque had been placed in 1971 by those who landed from HMS Tiger. John kindly had the replica made, giving me the original for 'The Rockall Club' archive, and had asked me to fix it to Rockall when I attempted to land for a second time in 2013. The second plaque was one I'd had made up myself to commemorate my first landing and the Queen's Jubilee in 2012.

It took me a couple of hours and two full batteries to carve the recess for John's plaque alone, the rock was so hard. Eventually the area was complete and smooth, and in addition I had managed to collect most of the chippings and dust on a mat below in order to provide yet more samples for St. Andrew's University. Just before 1600 the VHF crackled into life, and as I moved back to the RockPod to grab it, I looked to the southern horizon to see a couple of the ubiquitous trawlers, but also what appeared to be a boat-less wake between them.

I quickly responded to the 'Mary Slim', on Channel 16, switching to Channel 11, who confirmed that this wake was them, but as they had such a slim profile head on and the boat being silver-grey, it would be difficult to see the vessel itself until it got closer. I had previously agreed with their PR representative that I would take some photos and video of them as they rounded Rockall on their record-breaking speed attempt from Portland and back. In addition, they had agreed to take images of me on the rock from their boat. So, I grabbed my cameras and moved onto the patio and then up to the summit to take photos and filming some video, trying to get reference points of Rockall in the foreground so that it was clear that she was here and not just out in any bit of ocean.

I saw the flash of their camera several times, and hoped that they had got some good shots. We talked briefly via radio and waved, but then they were gone, being here probably for a maximum of ten minutes. I had hoped that they might stay a little longer as I had been looking forward to their visit, and perhaps come much closer so that I could see faces and we could shout to one another, but they were on a deadline with a record to set, so it was understandable that they didn't hang around. Not even the offer of a cup of tea would tempt them!

Once they had left, I cleared up the drill and kit I'd been using, as the temperature had started to drop and the air felt moister, indicating either that it was going to rain or at least I'd had the best of the weather for the day. In any case, having restarted the wind turbine, as I'd used a lot of power recharging the drill batteries, it was then around the time I now usually clamber back inside the pod to commence my evening routine of admin, checking forecasts, supper, reading and sleep. I would leave drilling the bolt holes for the plaques to another day.

This evening checking my emails meant I got the sad news that Niall Iain MacDonald's quest to row the Atlantic solo from New York to Stornoway had met an early end when he injured his back and had requested rescue. Niall Iain and I had been communicating for a number of years as we both organised our expeditions in parallel, suffering setbacks and fund raising issues at similar times. He loaned me the back-up solar panels I have with me on this expedition, which had been removed from his boat during her refit, and we had met when we were both successful finalists in the Kukri

Adventure Scholarship in 2013. I even had one of his 'NY2SY' support stickers on the RockPod in a gesture of solidarity, as we would both be out in North Atlantic at the same time. I'm glad he's safe, and hope his boat is recovered quickly.

Day 12 – 16th June

A bit of a change in scenery today, with the mist being very close in so that my view is restricted to a maximum of fifty metres in any direction. This is a stark change from the norm, when I can usually see to the horizon, unless it's bad weather. It's still quite bright though, and I think it must have rained in the night as the rock and surface of the pod are wet, unless this is just due to the amount of moisture in the air.

My first task was to plot the rock dust and water samples I've collected so far, for St. Andrew's University, onto the only topographic map of Rockall. I also intend to take some further water samples from any pools I come across as I move further around the rock, and will also collect rock samples from a variety of points across Rockall. In addition, I've started to plan how I might draw a scale plan of the summit plateau and its features, which should be helped by the fact that there are several remnant drill tracks across the top, which are parallel, from when the summit cone was blown off in 'Operation Tophat' in 1971, and will help me form a grid to work from. In addition, I've started to think about transect paths for the magnetic deflection measurements that Tim Raub has asked me to take for the University.

Also this morning, I finished the first of my seven, twenty five litre jerry cans of water. Assuming that I drink today what I decanted this morning, which I will, that means that I've averaged about 2.1 litres per day since I got here. This is slightly lower than I estimated, at 2.5 litres per day, and what is recommended, and there have been days where I've drunk three litres because of the temperature. However, I've not been dehydrated at any point, so am not worried and will continue to monitor my consumption. The added bonus is that the empty container can now go outside the pod, which means that I will have more space inside.

In any case, I have more than enough water with me for the sixty days. This year I decided to bring all I would need, plus extra, which was a departure from my plan last year when I had brought just enough water, five twenty-five litre jerry cans, plus a desalinator and a rainwater catchment kit that I had built myself from a poncho, funnel, and a length of tube. In the passing year I had decided that the issues associated with collecting sea water and the risks were potentially too great, the desalination unit was bigger and took up more space inside the RockPod than I had expected, and so I had decided that it would be better to just bring the extra weight of more fresh water, and put up with having less space in the pod for a while. The desalinator had been returned to the sponsor who donated it after last year's attempt, I brought my rainwater catchment kit just in case, as it weighed little and took up next to no space, and it meant that my satellite communications kit now fitted under the shelf inside the pod, where the desalinator would have been.

Moving the water canister inspired me to have a bit of a rearrangement of my kit barrels too. I clipped the water carrier to the outside of the pod in a temporary location (I suspect I'll have to move it to some other location once there's more than one out there). It had also become clear over the past few outings from the RockPod that two of my barrels, numbers seven and two, could be moved from immediately below the hatch, where they were forming a double row of drums, to spaces at either end of the line of barrels. In this way, I would have slightly more room to move along the back of the pod, which was my main route from one end of Hall's Ledge to the other, on a slightly more level surface.

In addition, having created a 'bin barrel' some days ago from drum number 10, I was now in the position of needing a drum designated for kit and equipment that I had used or was likely to be superfluous to requirements, but which was taking up space in the pod. This included a book I'd read, extra cartridges of resin which I was unlikely to need, and eventually my dirty clothing bag would join them too.

With there being no views to look at today, and with the mist sometimes coming in to around forty metres, there was a calm air about the place. There was a slight wind, just enough to turn the turbine, but next to no swell, at a very long period. Also there were no waves; the sea was still enough for the wind to ripple the surface. Not quite mirror calm, but not far off it. I had heard what I suspected was the minke earlier in the day, but had not been able to see it; it usually cruises past about one hundred and fifty metres to the West; but this afternoon it came within thirty metres of the South side of the rock, and I stood and watched it circling something for around fifteen minutes.

Having carved out the recesses for the new plaques yesterday, I decided this afternoon's job would be to drill the holes for the bolts. Not a difficult job, but cleaning out the holes was made more difficult by the fact that the rock seems to be holding a lot of moisture within it, suggesting that it is at least partly porous. This was particularly evident when brushing the surface of the recesses clean, or when trying to blow the dust out of the holes which came out as a paste when I used the drill bits to scrape the hole clean. For this reason I have decided to allow the holes and faces of the recesses to dry out over the next few days, and will leave fixing the plaques in place until a warm dry day, when I also plan to dry out my ropes and some other pieces of kit which I thought had gone into the drums dry after the landing, but seem to be giving off condensation within the drums.

Finally, I looked about for some suitable and easily accessible sections of rock to take samples from for St. Andrew's University in the future. I then took some specific photographs of the summit and the light housing, that members of the Greenpeace team had requested, in order that they could try and work out why their replacement light had succumbed to the ravages of the North Atlantic, when it had been designed to withstand the worst that the sea could throw at it.

Day 13 – 17th June

I woke up this morning with a slight feeling of what I could only describe as regret at being here, and waking up in the RockPod yet again. I'm sure this won't be the last time I have this feeling, and it passed quickly. I just have to make sure that this type of negativity doesn't creep in too often or stay around too long.

The sea was even calmer today, and I can't imagine it could get any more still out here. There was no wind nor waves, and a very slight swell, so that the birds on the water looked like they were on a pond rather than the open ocean. As it was so calm, it felt an obvious day to carrying out some of the measuring tasks I wanted complete, so after breakfast I drew up a plan of the light housing and also of the fall-line down the South face from the summit to Hall's Ledge. My policy is not to go up onto the summit if the turbine is moving, which it wasn't this morning, as I think this is the most likely source of serious injury for me: getting hit in the head by the spinning blades. I do have a helmet with me, and could wear that up there if necessary, but as I would be moving around a lot, and back and forth, to collect the measurements I needed, I thought it was best to do it on a still day.

One of the trawlers came particularly close before I left the pod this morning, perhaps because the sea was so calm. Through the binoculars I identified it as PD120 'Harvest Hope', which is the boat that has been sounding its horn as it passes, and one of the crew has been posting photos of me on Twitter. I watched them watching me through the binoculars, and even traded a wave which boosted my morale a tad and brought a smile to my face. I did consider talking to them on the VHF, but eventually decided against it, as I think too much human contact may stir some longing to be home, and also I'd like to save that treat for when I really need it.

I had noticed this morning that a single puffin had landed just below the pod which, although I have seen them flying past, is the first time I've seen one land. I managed to take a few good photos, and was about to try and capture some video of it before it disappeared again. However, as I was preparing to leave the pod, I caught out of the corner of my eye a flash of a very small bird as it darted away, obviously surprised by my emergence. I couldn't identify it, except that it was dark and the size of a sparrow or wren, but will be keeping an eye out for it again. I think there's a wren which is endemic to St. Kilda, but can't imagine it is this far out, particularly as the wind has been low and in the wrong direction for the past few days.

Once I was out of the pod, I took a couple of photos of the fall-line I was using to measure the height of the cliff for my records and then quickly measured the distances between the various markers along it, which included an old bolt, a rock core hole, and a couple of Greenpeace's anchors. The majority of this line was arguably vertical, but the lower section was angled and so I estimated the two significant changes in slope with my compass. It will require a bit of GCSE trigonometry later for me to work out the actual total height of this face above the ledge.

I then moved up to the summit and measured the various facets of the light housing, height, circumference, orientation, thickness of the shell, distance from the edges, etc. These may be of use to someone at some point, but if nothing else can be entered into The Rockall Club's archive of this place. I'm hoping that I will be able to obtain copies of the original design drawings from The Northern Lighthouse Board, not only for the archive, but also for comparison with my own observations. As luck would have it, just as I completed my survey of the housing, the wind picked up and the turbine started to spin, so I headed back down to the RockPod for lunch.

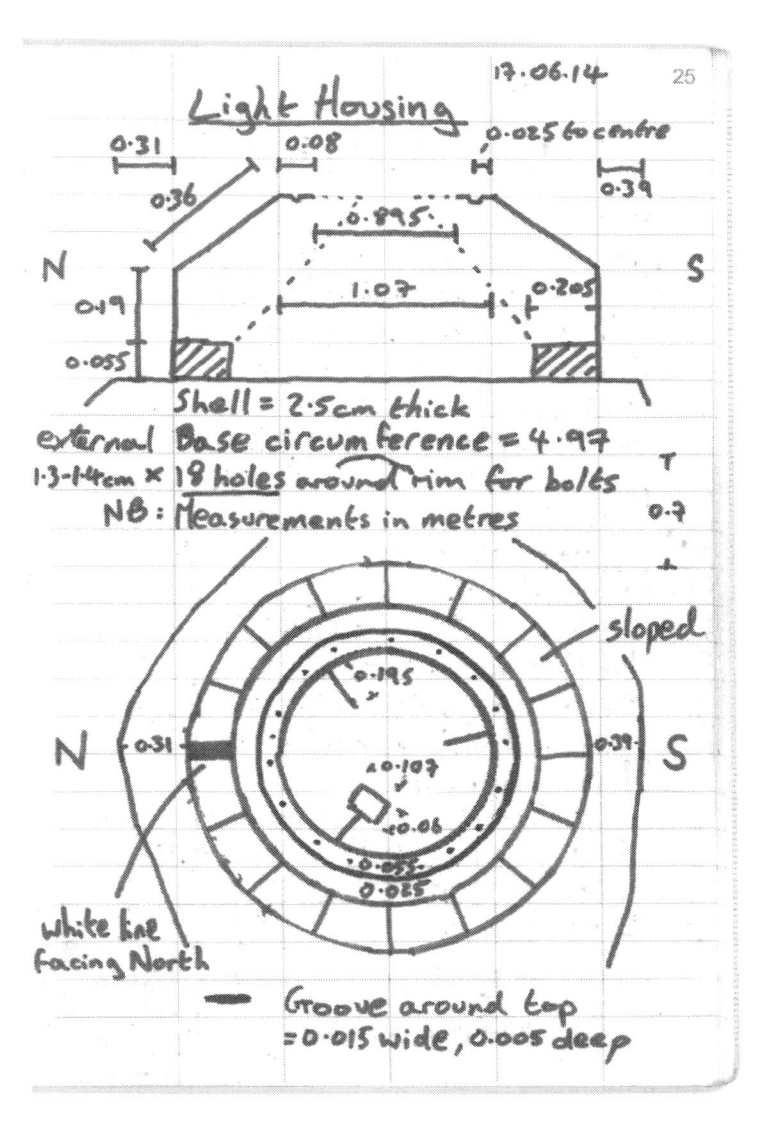

I dragged lunch out for as long as I could, and in the process finished my first gas canister, provided by my sponsor Calor, which is not at all bad as I managed to get two or three boils every day for twelve and a bit days out of it. I've brought ten canisters with me, based on calculations on burn times that I did at home, so I have more than enough to see me through, twice! I then finished reading the research report I started the other day, before heading back out to carry out some more measuring work, this time on the metal frame which formed the housing for a solar panel to power the light beacon, and is affixed to the south face above Hall's Ledge.

Apart from the obvious reason for carrying out all these small tasks of measuring and sample collection, to keep me and my mind busy each day, during the course of planning the expedition I had become very interested in the fascinating history surrounding Rockall and those who have landed in this remote spot. I set up 'The Rockall Club', to which I referred earlier, partly as somewhere to record all the facts I'd 'discovered' during my research, and partly to act as a repository for information regarding Rockall.

It was also with this in mind that during my time here I hoped to record any and all features of the place for future reference. This means photographing and measuring plaques, fixings, the light housing, etc. as well as drawing and measuring features such as the summit plateau, south face, Hall's Ledge, and conducting my GNSS survey of the height and position of the rock. Luckily, for such a small place, there is a lot of history to record.

Day 14 – 18th June

This morning started late, around 0920, and was characterised by loose bowels. Not a good thing at home, let alone out here. I'm hoping, however, that it is due to the lentil soup I had last night for supper rather than any intestinal issues. The weather is a bit brighter than it has been for the past few days, with patches of blue sky evident through the main hatch as I look skyward. I have managed to set a new record for breakfast of around two hours, which passed fairly quickly, demonstrating that I really am getting used to the slow pace of life here.

I decided it was about time I started doing some proper exercise, having previously messed about with the Thera-band that I brought with me to allow me to train in a semi static position within the RockPod. Today, however, I went about devising an all-around body work out with the band, which again will not only take up time to do, but will also keep me in reasonable shape for when I actually need strength for lowering the RockPod and my equipment off the rock and down climbing at the end of the expedition. There is of course the added, and hopefully un-needed, benefit that should I fall at any point, I should be strong enough to haul myself back up the rock.

Having finished that task, I went outside to brush down the plaque recesses and check whether they were any dryer, which they were. However, I thought that they could be smoothed down better and one of them needed to be a little deeper; but before I could start work I noticed clouds and what looked like rain coming in from the West. It looked like there was sunshine following behind, and so I retreated back to the pod for ten minutes while the shower passed through. Following that, it brightened up and I completed half an hour's work on the recesses, and am now much happier with how the plaques sit within them. A beep of my watch and a grumble in my stomach indicated that it was lunchtime, which I have pushed back until two o'clock as I'm having breakfast so late and taking so long to finish it.

The afternoon was uneventful, as I suspect more to come will be. I started reading 'Mr. Nice' using the Kindle software on my Ergo laptop. I would like to read more at home, but never seem to have the time or there's always something more productive to do, and when I have read in the past, it's generally been non-fiction: autobiographies, mountaineering and polar expedition books. I now have the time, and am breaking myself back in easily with this story, but hope that I might progress to some of the classics later in the expedition.

Day 15 – 19th June

Today is an important milestone as its two weeks since I landed on Rockall and fifteen days into the expedition: a quarter of the way through. Thinking about this, I allowed myself to look forward to other milestones to come, which I had previously tried not to do, in case the time I have left here becomes overwhelming. However, fifteen days means that its only five days until twenty, which marks one third of the way through the expedition, but perhaps more importantly is half way to the solo occupation record that I'm aiming for. If I didn't respect Tom McClean enough anyway for being out here for forty days in a plywood box, the fact that he managed that time without modern satellite communications is in my view astounding.

After twenty days, there's not much to celebrate until thirty, which will be half way though and only ten days to the solo record. Then come the records, forty days and forty-two for a group, followed by forty-five days being three quarters of the way there, and then I'm into the home straight. But enough of that…

I'd read somewhere before I left that an experiment to test how people would cope with a manned tripped to Mars, noted that the subjects slowed down to fit their required daily tasks to the time they had to complete them in, rather than rushing to get as much done in as short a time as possible, as we generally do in our daily lives. This appeared to be an unconscious reaction to having more time and less to do each day. I had hoped that the same would occur for me out here, and it appears that it is to some extent, although perhaps, because of that study, I am more aware of my state and so am forcing myself to slow down somewhat. Either way, I seem to be sleeping later, today I woke up about 0930, although I am still bedding down around 2200 (perhaps not falling asleep until after 2300). In addition, what daily tasks I have, eating, personal admin, etc. are definitely taking longer; but I am certainly forcing myself to complete one task at a time rather than doing things between sips of tea for example. The experiment continues.

This morning, after breakfast, I cut my nails which seem to be growing faster out here; this is the second time I've had to cut them in two weeks, and I also combed my hair and beard. Someone had once pointed out to me on a multi-day exercise with the OTC, how combing your hair just lifts the spirits a bit and makes you feel cleaner or more civilised for some reason. I suspect it's a subconscious link, like me not wearing a watch: I comb my hair when I'm at home after showering, as part of getting ready for the day; therefore, if I comb my hair, I'm ready for the day. I certainly felt cleaner and more civilised afterwards, and it had the added benefit of stopping an itch I've had on the side of my head.

The weather is pretty much the same again, and although I've not seen a synoptic chart, I suspect that I'm under a fairly stable weather system as the wind direction has stayed constant for a couple of days this time, the temperature has been twelve to thirteen degrees centigrade, and the wind hasn't got much above fourteen miles per hour for several days. It's forecast to be the same for the coming week too. In terms of my wellbeing, it's pretty much perfect, neither too hot nor too cold and not wet. However, it doesn't make for much mental interest.

I continued reading 'Mr. Nice' for much of the morning, and was pleased to find that reading passed the time quickly. After lunch, the weather improved and became warm and dry with blue skies, just the weather I'd been awaiting in order to finish a few jobs (and as it turned out, start some new ones!). The first thing was to unpack my two larger, un-numbered drums, which had not come with me on my failed landing last year, but which I'd introduced to the plan in order to house my large battery and the wind turbine, which had previously been in dry bags, and which had holed without even leaving the boat.

These barrels were hastily repacked after I landed, with my ropes, climbing hardware, dry suit and boots; none of which were properly dry. Although I had tried to air them before packing them away, they were generating condensation within the drums. The ropes I spread out in the sun and breeze on 'The Patio' with the dry suit hung across the row of taught ratchet straps behind the RockPod. I then mopped out any moisture I could from the drums with a sponge and left the whole lot to dry out while I got on with other things.

> HMS ~~~~ 1975
> Lt Cdr. Smith B.J.RN
> AA- Ellson A.R.
> POET Lenoir M.
> LEM(A) Wilson D.W.
> LA(PHOT). Dobson B.R.
> MR. A.Miller I.G.S.
>
> REPLICA J.COULL 2013

The main dry day job was to resin fix the two plaques for which I had previously carved the recesses. The mounting positions were dry and the bolt holes were as dry as I thought they were ever going to be, so I got on with it. All was pre-planned and went smoothly with, thankfully, the resin cartridge I'd opened to fix the wind turbine base, still in usable condition. The plaques resined into position, there were a few small gaps around the sides and behind the bolt heads where I thought water might get in and corrode the fixings, so I filled these with more resin and ran around the edges of each plaque to provide a good seal to the rock. This then gave me the idea of doing the same to some of the in-situ plaques in order to perhaps help extend their life here. To that end, I also sealed around the edges of the Lochaber District Council plaque commemorating Tom McClean's residency here, on the south facing cliff above Hall's Ledge, and the plaque dedicated to the landing from RFA Engadine, which is on the 'plaque wall'.

I decided not, however, to give the 'Light Beacon' plate on the plaque wall the same treatment for a number of reasons. The first is that if ever a replica of the 1955 annexation plaque is brought back to Rockall, it seems to me that the ideal place for it would be at the top of the plaque wall in place of the Light Beacon plaque, whose recess might provide part of that needed for the Queen's plaque, and so cut down the amount of work and time needed to install it there. Secondly, as mentioned previously, this plaque was one of a matching pair, and so both probably don't require preserving. Thirdly, the plaque wall plate was missing one bolt of four, as was the matching plaque on the summit (where the light beacon was actually located), so my thinking was that the plaque on the top of the rock should be sealed around, with perhaps one of the bolts from the other plaque being used to replace the missing one on the summit, thereby securing its future.

I therefore cleaned around the summit plaque in preparation, having put the resin gun away, and attempted to clean out the hole where the missing bolt would have been, and from which, I had assumed, like the plaque below, the bolt had somehow come out to be replaced with dirt and guano. Unfortunately, this was not the case, and it appears that just the bolt head has sheared off. In any event, I cleaned around it as much as I could, with my thinking being that I will go back and try and remove the beheaded bolt at some future point, and seal around the plaque then.

Day 16 – 20th June

I popped my head out of the RockPod at about 0940 this morning, just after I had woken up, to see that the Harvest Hope was very close to my South and heading East fast. I had an inkling that something must be different so raised them on Channel 10 on the VHF. Sure enough, they were heading home, and were taking a last swing by to get a better view of my set up and honk their horn in salute. We had a brief chat over the radio, in which I wished them a safe journey home and thanked them for their support. They in turn wished me luck and promised to spread the word about the expedition. Watching them head towards the Eastern horizon, I had a small pang of disappointment that they were away home and I was not, and thought about the moment when I see Orca 3 appearing at a similar point out there, heading this way to pick me up.

Most of the morning I spent reading and exercising with the Thera-band, before checking emails just before lunch, via the Inmarsat BGAN unit. I needed to get a phone number that I was to call NBC on at two o'clock in order to discuss some specific video shots they wanted for a piece they're intending to air about the expedition, with Ben Fogle. The conversation went well on the IsatPhone2 and we organised that I would download some video I had shot, and then have a Skype interview with Ben next week, which should hopefully be great PR for the expedition in the USA, and will hopefully be syndicated to ITN in the UK too.

I read for much of the afternoon, but when the wind dropped for a while I was out of the pod in a flash as I wanted to check that all the resin I'd applied yesterday had set properly, which it had, take some photos of the newly installed plaques and brass OS survey marker, do a bit of filming for NBC for the shots they wanted that I didn't have, and finish off my exercises with some calf raises and squats outside. Interestingly, at the end of the day, just I was settling in for the evening, the VHF crackled into life with a yacht speaking to one of the trawlers to verify the position of its nets.

Sometime later, a small light blue catamaran appeared in front of me. I looked through the binoculars but they made no attempt to communicate and seemed oblivious to my presence on the rock. They turned South shortly afterwards, and as I ate my supper I watched as they too, just as Harvest Hope had this morning, disappeared towards the horizon.

Day 17 – 21st June

It is another much quieter day today. The wind has picked up a bit, which has made it fairly cool to be outside, and the sea is getting choppy. There are very few boats about, and I have only seen one all morning. Whether this is because they've moved on, gone home ahead of the winds tomorrow (forecast 25 mph, gusting to 30 mph), or just finished fishing for this trip, I don't know. There are also a lot more birds today. The gannets still seem to have abandoned the rock, although I have seen one or two cruising past. However, there are a lot more puffins and a large raft of maybe up to eighty Manx Shearwaters has appeared. I spent a while watching their smooth flight as they cruised amongst the waves, not sure how they got so close without touching the water. A Bonxie (Skua) and a couple of common terns also appeared briefly, and I wondered whether this sudden change in the bird life has something to do with a precursor to the coming higher winds.

Much of the morning was spent reading, although I did attempt to upload some video for NBC, which failed for some reason; I will try again this evening. In the afternoon it cleared up and the sun came out for a while. I decided that I really should get out and about, particularly as I may not be able to tomorrow if the winds are too high. I did a few exercises out on the patio, which I won't be able to do if I am pod-bound tomorrow, and decided to measure all the plaques on the rock. There are now five: the 'light beacon' plaque on the summit, its matching pair on the 'plaque wall' along with the RFA Engadine, replacement HMS Tiger, and my 2012 plaque, and the Tom McClean plaque on the South Wall.

Having completed that task quickly, and having the necessary equipment out of the pod, I went on to measure the ramp, patio, east and west steps at either end of Hall's Ledge, and made an attempt at measuring the extent of the flattest part of the ledge itself. Certain assumptions have to be made, as the flattest section is not a regular shape, is sloped, undulates and is of course partially covered by my pod. Defining its North, East and West extent is fairly easy, but the southern edge is very irregular and arbitrary positions for the 'edge' have to be decided. For good measure, I also measured the distances between the four new fixings I had placed for the straps going over the deck of the RockPod, which roughly define the flattest rectangular area on the ledge, with the exception of the south-eastern most fixing which is down in a small gully.

It was actually really nice to be out of the pod, and the wind was not too strong, so I spent some time watching the birds and the minke. I also spotted three seals together, which confirmed my suspicion that there were at least three, as I have started to notice a difference in head shape when I see the individuals on their own. I suspect one is a female, as it has a much slimmer more 'feminine' head. The other two are obviously bigger and stronger, and I'm therefore assuming they're males.

Another job for later in my occupation, which I came up with at home while thinking of things to do, and as a result of my recce in 2012, is to take a moulding of Tom McClean's carving of his name in the rock. I have not seen mention of this in any of the literature on Rockall that I had read before I came, and it was quite a surprise to see it when I landed two years ago. For part of my collection of Rockall memorabilia, I had decided to try and take a moulding of this carving, so that I could reproduce it at home. I will be using latex, which needs as clean a surface as possible, and so I took the opportunity of a dry spell to scrub down the area and the carving with one of the stiff brushes I had brought with me.

Before I spent the rest of late afternoon and evening inside the RockPod, as the wind had picked up and it started to rain, I looked for a suitable location on the summit for some sort of standard sized base plate to be fixed, which could be used by any future expedition for anchoring a wind turbine or radio aerial. My weather station is saying that it is still around thirteen degrees, but with the wind chill it feels much colder, especially with the amount of moisture in the air and the fact that if I pop my head out it is very quickly wet from all the rain.

Day 18 – 22nd June

I woke again, at what now appears to be my natural waking time here, after nine. I'd expected to wake up to high winds, but the morning seemed perfectly pleasant, with a gentle south westerly breeze and relatively clear skies. I though perhaps that the high winds that were forecast had come through overnight, and I'd experienced the start of them before bed last night. However, they were forecast to get stronger as the day progressed, so in a break from the norm I had my breakfast fairly quickly and then set about some tasks outside the pod in case the weather deteriorates.

I still had some files to upload for NBC, so I started those going before emptying the latrine down 'Gardyloo Gully', which I had thought apt to name after the gully of the same name on Ben Nevis, and then photographed and recorded all the stainless steel Collinox anchors which had been left by Greenpeace and added to by me. I also noted where the few 'Raumer' hanging plates are, and noted where I had put the five stainless steel pulleys that I intend to leave here to assist others in the future. I decided yesterday that the best place for a fixed base plate was actually where my wind turbine currently stands, and that being so, the four 'Raumer' plates I had placed to tether the guy lines to were in the perfect position for guying any future turbine or aerial, so I recorded those in greater detail. My thinking is now that a standard scaffold foot plate, bolted to the rock and in stainless steel would be ideal, as then anyone can insert a standard length of scaffold pole and affix their turbine or aerial to that.

I had decided before I came, that if I could I would try and make landing equipment on Rockall easier. I don't, however, want the difficulty of landing people and the climb to the summit to be lessened as that might encourage more people, and those without the requisite climbing experience, to attempt to land, which would endanger not only them, but potentially any crew who brought them out here and potentially also the Coastguard.

However, I don't see a problem with doing small things to help out once someone had completed the main challenge of getting to and landing on Rockall. Along the same lines as the scaffold base plate idea, I had also thought to bring with me some standard scaffold ring anchor sockets. I'm still thinking where to place these, with the idea being that anyone landing in the future could just screw in the ring anchors, thread a scaffold pole through, and have a gibbet arm sticking out over the cliff edge to use to bring equipment up[24]. A contact at Greenpeace has hinted that they may replace their broken light, and I'm aware that amateur radio enthusiasts would like to come and 'activate' Rockall for longer than has been achieved in the past.

In the early afternoon the wind picked up and the rain came in for a while. I re-read Basil Hall's account of the first landing on Rockall in 1811, which was an interesting exercise, as although I'd read it a few times before, actually being here and recognising the landmarks he talked about, made it all the more real. I was actually able to imagine the sailors and scientists of the day clambering around and recording aspects of the rock. I wondered if their

---

[24] In the end, I decided not to fix these anchor sockets as there is probably already too much metalwork on the rock.

sketches are in the National Maritime Museum in Greenwich. After lunch the rain had stopped, but the wind was still too cool to warrant going outside the pod if I didn't have to, so I settled in and finished off 'Mr. Nice'. The final paragraph brought tears to my eyes, and reminded me, if I needed it, how much I am missing my family, and particularly my son Freddie.

Soon after I'd finished the book I heard the minke surfacing and blowing close to the rock and saw that it was within ten metres of the base of Rockall on the south side, right in front of me. I managed to get a few good photographs of its dorsal fin and some video of it surfacing and blowing, and could even see its white fin and markings on its side as it moved beneath the water. At the same time I noticed a green plastic carrier bag floating past just below the surface. This is the second I've seen since I came here, and just goes to show, if the traces of rope and wire in the birds' nests on Rockall didn't, how far our rubbish can travel if discarded thoughtlessly. The shearwaters and the skua had also reappeared, and I watched as it harassed the other birds for them to release their hard won meals.

I spent most of the afternoon reading, finishing 'Mr. Nice' and starting on Ice-T's autobiography. Having checked and replied to a few emails around six o'clock, I heard more blowing from the minke close to the rock. I watched it for a while and was intrigued how it breathed a few times and next time I saw it, it could be quite a distance away and moving back towards me. Then the obvious was made very clear when two whales surfaced close together!

Oddly, having not seen them together before, they were both close to Rockall and each other for a while, so I wonder if the second one is a recent arrival, drawn perhaps by a food supply which is currently in closer to the rock. Either way, one whale close in was great, but two was amazing, I continued to watch until they disappeared, before having supper.

Day 19 – 23rd June

I didn't sleep well last night, and was up well after midnight. In some ways it was nice to be awake at that time as I could see Rockall in a whole new light, literally. Due to its northerly location and the time of year it wasn't properly dark, but due to the cloud cover it wasn't light either. The wind had dropped and the sea was relatively calm. The only noise, apart from the waves hitting the rock, was the distant chug of a trawler engine which also had its lights on as it worked away through the night. I watched it for a while and took in the night air, before reading for half an hour and eventually dropping off. The problem is that because I'm not using much mental energy, my mind is racing when I go to bed, planning the order in which my kit will come off the rock, last minute tasks before leaving, and how I'm going to celebrate once back to shore.

As a result of the late night, I didn't wake until 0940, and then only because the VHF crackled into life with a couple of trawlers speaking to each other. I dozed, and finally rose just after ten; I didn't have anywhere to be. My only deadline each day is to set off my SPOT Messenger before midday to say that I'm 'OK'; although I'm sure my family would feel that the earlier I set it off, the better.

Today heralded another change of underwear, which I have changed since last time I mentioned it, but the novelty wore off pretty quickly, although it is nice to have clean socks and pants on. I'm actually not wearing socks very much, probably not even a full day's wear in six, as I don't wear them in the pod because there's no need to and I want to let my feet breathe following an early episode of athletes' foot. I had a full bag of rubbish too, and as it looked like rain on the horizon, after breakfast I carried out some chores outside the RockPod: rubbish into Barrel 10, washing into the bag in Barrel 3, etc. I also needed some more toilet roll as I'd run out this morning, and while finding that, I brought in another pair of underwear and socks for the next change, a clean T-shirt, to celebrate day 20 tomorrow, some rations, and another gas canister. Back in the pod, I turned my pillow case inside out in the hope of getting another ten days use out of it.

As I was finishing my morning cup of tea, back in the pod, I saw, for just a few seconds, on the small ridge above the plaque wall, a small brown bird, which looked very out of place here. It was all one colour, mottled brown like a thrush, but about starling sized, and when it flew off, it had similar shaped wings to a starling too. Its beak was short and dark, and I heard a bird call a bit later, which I assume must have been from this bird as it was not one I'd heard since I got here. I'm hoping it'll land close again, and I'll have my camera ready to get a photograph in order to help me identify it.

Following some more reading and lunch, I returned to watching the minke when they surfaced, and was pleased to see that they appear to now be swimming together, in parallel. I'm hoping this perhaps means that they might be about to mate. It's probably the right time of year, summer, and there's lots of food around here on the Rockall Bank, so that would be nice to see. After a while though, a pang of boredom surfaced, and so I finally started my Italian lessons, which I have been meaning to do for the past few days, but I hadn't previously been able to find the time! I completed the first ten minute lesson and test with a mark of 96%, which I'm happy with. I'm not surprised though as I've had some basic lessons before and spoken some Italian while travelling in Italy. We'll see how I get on with future, more advanced lessons.

Although they had gone quiet over the past few days, I had been asked by Severin Carrell at The Guardian to write a blog for their Scottish section. The Guardian had been very supportive last year, setting up a dedicated Rockall Solo web page and blog on their website for me, with some fantastic graphics and associated stories. Unfortunately, because of the impending referendum, Severin did not have the resources to provide the same coverage this year. However, he had said that if I could provide a blog with a 'hook' then he would publish it online. My hook was having been twenty days out here, and so in the afternoon I wrote a blog summarising the experience so far, highs and lows, etc. with a view to emailing it to him this evening for publication tomorrow on day twenty.

Late in the afternoon I became unusually cold, and couldn't warm my hands. I wrapped up and closed the side window in the RockPod, but to no avail; so I ended up having to make a cup of tea, which has had two benefits: the stove heated the pod a little and the tea heated me. I'm not sure what made me so cold, the day was no colder or windier than normal, but I had been stood up, with my top half out of the pod for a while watching and photographing the minke, so perhaps that was the cause. Or, perhaps it was because I somehow seemed to have got the split of my rations wrong yesterday, and so had less to eat today than normal and so less energy. In any event, a warm cup of tea and good clothing seemed to do the trick.

I was looking forward to going online tonight as I'd hoped to write a long email to my wife, and was also expecting a few responses to queries I'd sent out in the previous few days. However, the weather turned and it started raining soon after I'd logged on. Unfortunately the base unit for the BGAN (Broadband Global Area Network) unit is not ruggedised and so can't cope with the rain. If it's raining when you want to you use it, you're supposed to disconnect the base unit from the aerial, link them via a long cable, and keep the base in the dry; but this doesn't allow for a change in the weather mid-transmission. This meant that I had to rush through my emails, swiftly reading what I could, responding where I had to, and writing a very short message to my wife. It's forecast to rain for the next few days, so I'll have to get the long cable out.

Day 20 – 24th June

An important day, and one I have been looking forward to for a few days, with the combination of life becoming very slow and writing a blog yesterday, looking forward to today, meaning that I'd felt that I was here before I actually was. Twenty days means that I'm officially one third of the way through this challenge, half way to the twenty nine year old solo occupation record, and also three weeks into the expedition. I treated myself to a clean T-shirt and fleece top, the first for twenty days, and relished the smell of clean clothes and the fact that there wasn't a pervading whiff of body odour about the pod; the dirty clothes were consigned to barrel number 3 when I went out later on.

I woke up a bit earlier this morning, around 0840, having fallen asleep pretty quickly last night, probably because of the late night the one before. I was also hungry when I woke up, the first time since I've been here, which confirms that I got my rationing wrong yesterday or the day before. After breakfast, I read for a while, finishing in the process Ice-T's autobiography and starting Jay-Z's. I was due to check for an email around 1330 to see if I was to do a Skype interview with Ben Fogle for NBC this afternoon or tomorrow. If it was to be this afternoon I wouldn't have much time for anything else substantial. So, I decided to leave the RockPod for a while and collect some more samples.

Following the rain last night, the moss on the rock was bright green, and that's perhaps what motivated me. It is often much darker and unremarkable when dry. I had thought before I left to come here than one of the things I might miss the most was the bright green colour of plants. The colour of the moss was therefore a very welcome sight. In addition, I had checked last night the recording techniques that Tim Raub of St. Andrew's University had suggested I used, and noticed, which I had previously ignored as I didn't think that there would be any here, that he was keen for me to collect any samples of sand caught in crevices that I might see. Surprisingly, to me at least, one of the old rock sampling core hole in the back wall had been filled with what appeared to be sand.

I took my spare, round pointed knife and a couple of sample bags from one of the barrels and proceeded to scrape some moss samples into one of them from various parts of the rock, and where the moss looked different for any reason, in case there was more than one species present. In searching for suitable sample areas I suddenly notice a tiny red mite crawling over the moss, so dashed back to the pod to get the invertebrate kit (vial of alcohol and forceps) from the Hunterian Museum, and was successful in catching two of the mites for their interest[25]. I then returned to my planned collecting and scraped out some hardened sand from the core hole into another bag, getting quite a large sample in the process. I also noticed what I thought was a red lichen on the back wall. However, on further inspection, I saw a similar blue deposit too. My thinking is that this must be some remnants of the Union Jack that Tom McClean apparently painted here in 1985, as I've not read any other accounts of anyone painting this wall. I've not seen any photographs of the exact position of the flag, but will try and obtain one, and

---

[25] Appendix A

I will also take some paint scrapings back with me before they are lost forever to the sea.

I'm trying to do some exercise at least every other day, and as I was out of the pod, and potentially inside for much of the afternoon, I took the opportunity to do some squats and calf raises on the patio, before climbing back inside. I checked my emails as planned around 1300, only to discover that the plan had changed and instead we did a Skype test call, and arranged to do the interview tomorrow morning. While online, I took the opportunity to check and respond to emails that I had not been able to deal with last night due to the weather, and noted that Severin had very kindly published my blog on The Guardian website. It was raining at the time, but I had planned ahead and fitted the long cable to the BGAN which allowed me to keep the base unit inside the pod.

After lunch, I read for a little while as it was still raining, before doing some more Italian lessons and exercising in breaks in the weather. The minke were very active just down in front of the RockPod and in watching them this afternoon, I came to the conclusion that there are now at least three whales here, if not four or five. This is absolutely amazing to see, and I can only assume that they are gathering because of a good food supply or to mate. I know there are three as I've seen them surface in quick succession, in different locations and moving in different directions. I think there may be more due to the fact that 'other' whales surfaced shortly afterwards, some distance from the first three and I don't believe they could have swum that far in the time. I may be mistaken.

Day 21 – 25th June

Today has been a fairly quiet day, which I needed as I did not get to sleep until after 0200 this morning. My brain was not particularly active, but I was definitely awake. I've come to the conclusion that this might be due to drinking hot chocolate before going to bed, which recently has coincided with these nights of difficult sleep. I'm going to try and avoid it in the evenings for a while, as I generally do with coffee and tea after lunchtime, and see if that makes a difference.

Having said all that, I still felt I should set an alarm for 0900 as I had an online interview with Ben Fogle for NBC at 1000 and didn't want to miss that, particularly as I had quite a bit of setting up to do with the BGAN, webcam, video camera and moving things around inside the pod to accommodate the various angles required. As it happened, I woke around 0830 anyway and so the alarm was not needed. After breakfast and coffee, I settled in and we completed a twenty minute interview in two takes via Skype with me also recording on the video camera here, so that I can send higher resolution images to NBC for them to use. Ben was as pleasant as you would expect, particularly as he had apparently just walked in the door from filming in Alaska and so was no doubt very tired himself.

That took up much of the morning, and not feeling like reading and having been pod bound for most of yesterday, I got out and about before lunch to do the usual admin plus generally have a ponder and enjoy the milder, calmer weather. I got the odd sighting of the minke, but nowhere near as much activity as yesterday. After lunch I decided to do a few of the tasks I'd thought of over the past few days, and so went up onto the summit, measured the distances between the fixings up there and drew a rough sketch of the layout of the summit plateau, and I also stood up on top of the light housing and took a series of vertical photographs looking down onto its rim and the edge of the summit so that I can piece them together to get an accurate idea of the shape of that end of the ridge.

Following that, I descended back to Hall's Ledge and cut away the remnants of the rope, that the Belgians had left in the winter of 2012, from the East

Step as it was not only a potential trip hazard for me, but it also choked two of the Greenpeace fixings and a pulley I will be leaving in place. I didn't want to discard the old rope to the sea so have laid it aside until I can think what to do with it. If nothing else, I'll take it back with me to bin, but I half thought it might be good to re-tie it somewhere prominent as a marker of their landing.

Before supper I discovered that there may be an issue with one of the batteries for the BGAN satellite unit: the unit will not switch on when this particular battery is installed, and when I connected the DC cable to power it up, the display indicated that there was no battery. I have emailed Inmarsat to see if they have any ideas, but having checked the manual, unless its fully discharged, which I doubt, it looks like it may have failed which is not the end of the world, as I have two, but it does make life slightly more complicated.

I had a cold meal tonight for the first time as I didn't want to have a hot drink, as part of my experiment into what is keeping me awake. I therefore didn't need to boil any water, which I would also normally use to heat up my food. It was fine, and I already knew that the rations I'd brought with me could be eaten hot or cold. There was a lovely glimmer off the sea to the west as the sun started to set, the swell is higher again, maybe two to three metres, and the minke are cruising around. It is lovely and I fell privileged to be the only person here to witness the scene laid out before me.

Day 22 – 26th June

I slept much better last night, so perhaps it was the hot chocolate that kept me awake. I'll test the theory again tonight. Before I went to sleep I put the faulty battery for the BGAN on to charge, and went to sleep with nothing appearing to be happening. However I was pleased to see that this morning it was fully charged and the BGAN would start up on the battery alone. It had obviously become fully discharged without me realising, when I had both batteries connected, and so had taken a while to kick back into life.

There was blue sky over the top hatch when I first opened my eyes and it was a bright and sunny morning. This quickly reverted to type and became overcast, but with sunny breaks in the cloud. The wind had shifted around to the East and so I was fairly well sheltered from what my weather station was reporting were twenty mile per hour winds. More gannets had appeared, and along with them several Bonxies, who were harassing the gannets when they resurfaced from diving for fish right in front of the pod.

147

I was very stiff this morning when I got up. This is partly because of holding an awkward position leaning against my water tanks yesterday for half an hour recording the interview for NBC, after which I was already sore, but I suspect it may also be as a result of lying every night on a hard surface and being reclined for much of the day each day. One extra bit of kit I would bring, if I did this again, would be a proper sleeping mat. I had considered it during the planning for the expedition, but had reasoned that the foam matting on the floor of the pod would be sufficient and so I was better to save the space in the barrels that a mat would have taken up for something else.

It was forecast to get windier and wet in the afternoon, so in the morning, after breakfast, I did some exercises both inside and outside the RockPod. Then I collected some paint scrapings from what I'm assuming is the remnants of the flag Tom McClean painted while he was here, scrubbed out his carving a little more in preparation for taking a mould of it and cleaned out the black latrine bucket. Then I decided that as the wind was from the East, and so the wind turbine was pointing away from where I climb up to the summit, I could make a start on mapping out the plateau up there.

The summit plateau was created when the Royal Engineers blew the top off Rockall to facilitate the installation of a light beacon (now defunct), and there are still the parallel drill tracks across the top where the explosives were set. These nicely form the basis for a grid, and I managed to measure the width of these grooves and the distances between them before the wind started to pick up, as forecast. I started by measuring the width of the drill tracks, which are all four centimetres wide, give or take the odd millimetre, and then recorded the distance between the tracks from the Western most point on the summit up to the light housing. The next stage would have been to measure along the sides of the housing and beyond to the Eastern most point, but the wind picked up, a cloud bank was fast approaching and it felt like rain, so I retreated back to the pod.

Having spent most of the afternoon reading, during which time I finished Jay-Z's book 'Decoded' and started Steven Tyler's autobiography, because of the high winds (over thirty mph), around four o'clock I took a break to watch the birds hovering in the wind and see the sea at its roughest since I've been here. I suddenly spotted a small yacht approaching from the South. I watched as they were buffeted by the waves and although they were looking at me looking at them through the binoculars, they did not return my wave. Having passed by on the West side of the rock, the VHF came to life and I spoke with John Trythall who, along with his wife Janet, on their boat 'Jaywalker' had come out via a night's stop at St. Kilda, from the Outer Hebrides. It had taken them three days all told, and they expected to be heading to Northern Ireland on their return, due to the prevailing wind direction.

The afternoon was then fairly dull, and one that I had not been looking forward to for a while: high winds make it too cold to go outside without a good reason. I finished another couple of harmonica lessons from my book, before returning to read some more. By early evening I was even stiffer, and I suspect that I'm going to be very stiff and sore in the morning as a result.

Due to the weather, I decided to have a hot drink before bed and went for the hot chocolate. We'll see whether I'm still awake late again tonight.

Day 23 – 27th June

I woke to a glorious day and had slept well, so I'm not sure where that puts my hot chocolate theory. Bright blue skies, sun shine, and a fairly strong but not intolerable wind were the order of the day. It was the sort of sunshine that makes you squint and then sneeze! It really lifted my spirits and put an involuntary smile on my face. I had breakfast watching the gannets, who had returned overnight in some numbers, dive for fish, timing them as they hit the water to see how long they are under (four seconds) and learning when they were about to dive in order to try and get some photographs.

As the wind was still strong, the birds were able to use it to hover over Rockall and I got some nice shots of them from the side and underneath, as they glided by. A small brown bird appeared, I think probably bigger than the one I caught out of the corner of my eye a few days back. It was a bit damp and bedraggled to begin with, but soon dried out and looked like a young, brown starling. It was around for a while, picking at the piles of seaweed which lie here and there looking, I assume, for bugs to eat. I saw it later and it was wet again, so it's either found somewhere to bathe or it's been dodging the waves further down.

In the afternoon I read again for a few hours, before heading onto the wind dried rock to take photographs of the sea in the great light. I also took some of the RockPod from various angles, using the full length of my life line to enable me to get as wide an angle as possible, showing the pod in context with the rock, and to get below it down the south face. I also managed to get some great video of the waves crashing round the sides of Rockall and meeting on the other side in a maelstrom of foam and spray.

When it came to checking my emails in the evening, I saw that a reporter from The Sun had got in touch asking for an interview, and very efficiently suggesting a time this evening and another on Sunday morning for him to call me. I responded saying tonight would be fine, and bang on cue he phoned and we chatted for about half an hour. I'm hopeful he'll write a good piece, which will generate more followers and therefore more sponsorship for Help for Heroes.

Due to the interview, supper was an hour later tonight, around 2000. I had been getting worried about the connection between the gas canister and the stove as they didn't seem to be fitting as easily as they should. It being a high quality MSR stove, I put the issue down to the thread on the canister I was using wearing down, they are disposable after all, and decided to keep using it until it either it ran out or the thread failed. The thread failed this evening, but not on the canister, on the stove! I was very surprised because it's a very good make of stove and most if not all stoves which take a self-sealing screw-on canister have a standard thread. It appears that MSR stoves perhaps do not, and this may be the cause of the issue.

Annoyingly, I had considered bringing my old reliable MSR 'Pocket Rocket' with me as a backup, but had decided against it due to the fact that I had never had any issues with that MSR stove, and this new one was better quality; a decision I now regret. I fiddled with the stove for a while before deciding I was too tired do anything with it tonight. So I ate my dinner cold, which was fine, although resigning myself to the fact that all meals from now on may be cold, and a lack of morale giving hot drinks was a tad depressing.

Day 24 – 28th June

The first job this morning, before anything else, was to look at the stove with fresh eyes. I quickly confirmed that the thread on the stove's valve was the issue, and that it was not reparable. However, I also noted that the seal was still intact, and that the gas canister would now just push onto the valve. Therefore, I reasoned, if I could hold it tightly enough in place the stove may work. Elastic bands wouldn't be strong enough, and plasti-ties would have to be cut off every time a canister finished. There may also be issues maintaining the pressure with them to keep the canister and valve together.

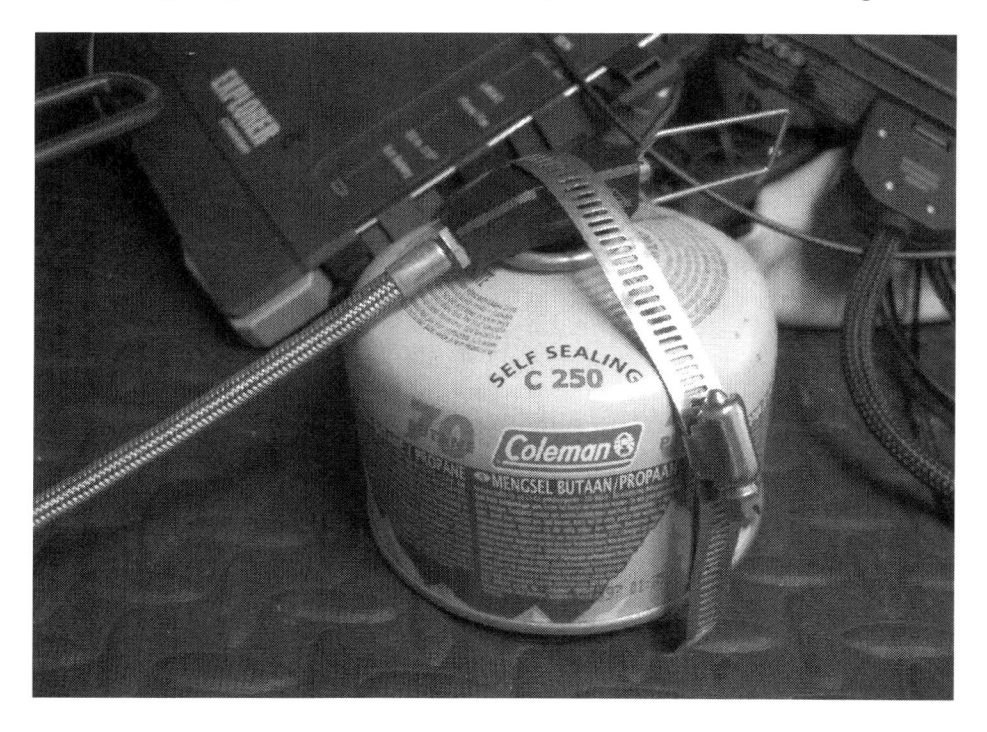

I then remembered that in Barrel 3 (spares and things I don't now need) I had two steel pipe clamps which came with the weather station to attach it to a mast, but which I hadn't used. These are regularly used to clamp pipes to gas apparatus, so I thought they might work in this instance, plus they have the advantage of being able to be tightened very tight with a screwdriver, but are also releasable to change the canister.

They were individually too short for the job, so I joined them together to form one band and then wrapped them around the canister and valve, tightening as I went until the valve was seated on the canister more firmly than if I had screwed it on. I then left the set up for a while, constantly listening and smelling for leaks, of which there were none, so after about five minutes I tested it, with all the windows and vents wide open – success! A great hot breakfast and cup of tea followed. I will have to look after the new stove set up so that it doesn't get knocked, and continually monitor for leaks, but I'm confident that this should last me now until the end of the expedition.

Next, the second water jerry can was finished this morning, so again I put the empty one outside which gives me even more room inside the pod. It's tricky finishing a can off as I would normally lie one down and put the other that I'm currently using on top to give me enough height with which to fill my two water bottles beneath from the tap. When the water level in the vessels becomes low, it has to be steeply tilted and when near empty I actually have to get the water can outside the top hatch of the pod and tilt it back inside in order to get enough of an angle to get the water out without spilling it. I have to be very careful at this stage, as although I don't mind losing a tiny bit of water, as I have more than enough at the current rate of consumption, I don't want to lose too much nor do I want to spill it into the pod. A funnel would be the ideal solution, however the one I brought with me as part of my rainwater collection kit, which I doubt I'll actually use, is too big to fit into the neck of my water bottles as I had not foreseen a need to use it in that way.

After all the in-pod admin was completed, I took some rubbish out and while out there prepared the exterior for the bad weather that is forecast to come. Tomorrow is supposed to be still and warm, the calm before the storm, but then the wind is forecast to build up through Monday, until it is in excess of thirty miles per hour on Tuesday, gusting closer to forty miles per hour, and remaining that way for several days, accompanied by rain. I planned for this sort of weather when I designed the RockPod, but so far I've been lucky. To prepare I brought into the pod further rations, loo roll, wet wipes and a change of underwear, just in case it's too windy to go out or too wet to open the barrels for a few days. My water is all in the RockPod anyway, so no preparation required there.

I then went up to the summit and checked the mast of the wind turbine for stability and the tension on the guy wires. They have already stood up to winds gusting over thirty miles per hour, but things slacken with time, and I decided that a couple of the guys could be tightened a little more which I did. Next I went around the pod and double checked the tension on the ratchet straps while also tidying up any spare lengths of strap, as experience has taught me that in high winds the worrying thing is the sound of the unknown flapping about and hitting the outside of your shelter. That completed, I used a length of chain I'd brought with me to strap down the two empty water containers, as they are very light and would easily catch the wind, and checked the straps holding the barrels to the pod and the rock. One of the larger barrels on the step at the West end of the pod was only tethered by one of its handles and was a bit too loose for comfort, so I threaded a climbing sling and karabiner through the other handle and clipped it back to the pod.

I spent much of the afternoon enjoying the weather, pondering and reading. In the late afternoon the Aalskere, one of the trawlers which has been here for a while from Kirkwall, drifted in to around one hundred metres from the rock, and while they were hauling in their catch I watched them through the binoculars. They then headed away South, not towards Kirkwall, but perhaps to other fishing grounds or a round-about route home. Neither was correct, she returned along the same heading a quarter of an hour later.

Before supper I went online to check my emails, send a few and more importantly to check the weather forecast. It looks like the winds at the moment will peak at gusts of around forty eight miles per hour during the night on Tuesday into Wednesday, today is Saturday. I was intrigued to know what this wind speed is on the Beaufort Scale, and so downloaded a copy to see that it is a 'Strong Gale'. That did nothing for my apprehension; ignorance is sometimes bliss; but too late now. I worried a little over supper, but then when I thought about it, the pod might get sprayed with sea water, but I won't get blown off the rock. I might even get buffeted a bit, but I shouldn't move. However, I do plan to take down the Help for Heroes banner at the back of the pod tomorrow, close to fifty mile per hour winds may be just too much for even that to take, and I'll go around the pod again, perhaps moving the dry bags and rope mat into a more sheltered position behind the RockPod.

Thinking about the prospect of very high winds over supper made me feel extremely apprehensive. I had a word with myself, went through everything I could do to prepare in my mind, and tried to think how fifty mile per hour gusts might affect me, the RockPod and my kit. By doing that I realised that there really wasn't much to worry about, particularly as the swell isn't forecast to be too high; although the waves may be up to four metres they are forecast to move round to the West by that point. I expect that the pod will get sprayed as the wind will be driving from the South West, which is straight at Hall's Ledge, head on, but I will be dry inside and the kit outside is all tied down and will, to some extent, be protected by being behind the pod. The wind flow may even part around Rockall, and I may find that I'll be sitting in a relatively calm zone. Anyway, I decided that I would be fine, the pod is not going to get blown away and that thought, along with the current external conditions, lifted my morale.

I had expected my evening to take the normal format, but when I poked my head out of the pod after supper I saw that it was very still, mild, and the sun was promising a spectacular sunset. After reading for a while, I decided that I really shouldn't miss this opportunity, and so got dressed and headed out to the top of the rock, where I sat for over an hour watching the sun slowly sink behind some low clouds and then into the ocean on the horizon, right up to the point that it disappeared altogether around eleven o'clock. I was hoping to the see the fabled green flash that I've heard about, which apparently can occur just after the sun disappears beneath the horizon due to the bending of the light, but unfortunately the conditions weren't right tonight. It was interesting, however, to note that the North side of the rock was bathed in sunlight right up until the point that the sun disappeared, but Hall's Ledge had been in shadow since around eight o'clock in the evening. I was in bed later than usual, but it was worth staying up for.

Day 25 – 29th June

I was hoping to wake up late today after a late night, but it was not to be, and I rose about 0845 to find a lovely day, as forecast. Low winds meant that the turbine wasn't turning, the sea was almost flat calm and it felt relatively warm.

Today I had planned that my main job would be to finish measuring and mapping the summit plateau, which I had started a few days ago, as long as the wind was low as forecast, which it was. I started by completing the measurement of the distances between the drill tracks. I then set up a central line along the length of the plateau and measured the length of the tracks either side of the central line, which proved a little tricky around the light housing, but I got round this, literally, by setting up offset lines either side of the housing, at known distances from the central line.

The Western end of the summit terminates in a point, so that was easy to record, but the Eastern end is rounded, and so I chose four distinct points on the curve, measuring the distance out to each from the last track line at that end of the ridge, and the distances between each one in order to describe the curve. I finished by measuring the distances of the sides of the light housing from the edges of the summit along each drill track it crosses, the position of the three main anchor points and the plaque from the central line, and finally the hole centres and bolt diameters of the four bolts left in place from Greenpeace's wind turbine.

Deciding I deserved a cup of coffee, I then returned to the pod and relaxed for a while. It's interesting to me that now, every time I light the stove I get an additional morale boost from the fact that I got it going again after it broke. I'm not sure how long the novelty will last, but it's good to have at this point. There was not much to do for the rest of the day, and I spent the remainder of the afternoon reading, pondering and watching the wildlife, including the small brown bird which I've decided, with the help of some suggestions by email, is a juvenile starling. He's a long way from home, but seems to be happy enough flying around and picking bits out of the gannets' seaweed nests. There should be fresh water for him here too, when it rains, as long as he finds shelter from the winds.

I did think to tie a loop of paracord around the external handle I use to get in and out of the pod, which will extend up to one of the handles of the main hatch when it's open. This means that if I do have to open the hatch when the winds are high, I can at least brace the hatch to stop it blowing back and breaking the hinge. My second gas canister ran out at supper time, so I needed to change that, which gave me the opportunity to check and retest the rigging I'd constructed with the pipe clamps. It's holding well.

Day 26 – 30th June

I woke early this morning, before eight, which is annoying as although I'd slept well, one of the best ways to cut down the time here is to sleep through it. Over the past few days the time has started to drag and I've felt a little bored a couple of times. This is partly because I have less and less to physically do, although there are some jobs, such as rock sample collecting and geomagnetism measurements to take, which I have not yet started. I'd always thought that this period from twenty days to half way at thirty days would feel slow as I willed myself to the half way point.

I suspect that the period from thirty to forty days will be the same, although I will then be on the downhill slope back home. Like running or climbing a mountain, where it's better not to think about reaching the end or the summit, it's better to enjoy the here and now. The end will eventually come when it comes, there's no stopping time. In addition, however, I have also been thinking about the bad weather that's due to arrive tomorrow, and thinking ahead, even two or three days, has a negative effect on your perception of time out here.

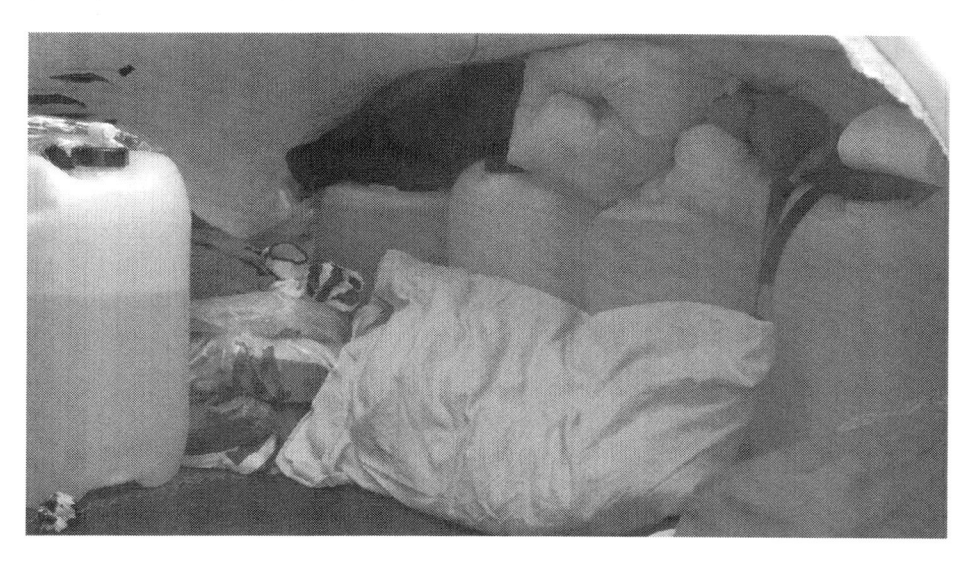

To kill some of that time before breakfast, I looked at the Ampair wind turbine instructions to double check that it would be able to withstand the coming winds. I was confident that it would be able to, but always better to check these things if you can. I needn't have worried: the maximum gusts forecast are currently forty eight miles per hour (Force 9, Strong Gale) and the 'Survival Wind Speed' of the turbine is in excess of seventy miles per hour (Force 12, Hurricane) – a well-made piece of kit. I also sterilised one of the water bottles I've been using to decant the jerry cans into for daily use and to monitor my consumption. It's clear and I think that the light has enabled some mould to grow in the bottle and inside the mouth piece. I used a chlorine tablet from the ration packs to clean the bottle and will boil the mouth piece next time I have a hot drink.

Personal hygiene out here is key to surviving the expedition. Rockall is not a clean environment, with the rock being covered in guano, and there's no fresh water supply. My drinking water is from a tap on Harris and so has been treated to potable standards; I have also brought enough sterilization tablets with me to treat my entire water supply if I had to. My food is sterile, being boil in the bag, so food poisoning should not be an issue as long as I can keep my plastic spoon, mug and water bottles clean. I eat out of the bags, which saves on having to clean a plate or bowl too. The mug and spoon I clean regularly with eco-sensitive biodegradable wet wipes, of a type recommended to me by the ocean rower Sarah Outen, as I cannot afford to use my fresh water for cleaning kit or washing myself.

I also use the wet wipes to periodically clean myself in key areas, and also have a couple of bottles of anti-bacterial hand gel with me, which I use every time I get back into the RockPod from being outside, before I eat, and after going to the toilet. Hopefully this regime means that I will continue to have no issues. It has, however, occurred to me that having two months away from other people may mean that my immune system is not as strong or as 'up to date' as it would have been had I been at home and work for this period of time. So, it will be interesting to see if I go through a period of illness once I return to civilisation.

It ended up being a fairly busy morning. The first jobs were to put the empty gas canister in the trash, and then double check what was in Barrel 2 as I couldn't remember how much of my consumables were still in there, if any. There were none. I took down and packed away my morale giving Help for Heroes banner in preparation for the coming winds; then I emptied the latrine bucket, and while doing so spotted a likely flake of rock to practice rock sampling on. I wanted to practice so I knew how hard the rock is and how easy it is to get samples before I'm half way down one of the faces. Small chunks broke off easily, so I collected a few samples for St. Andrew's University.

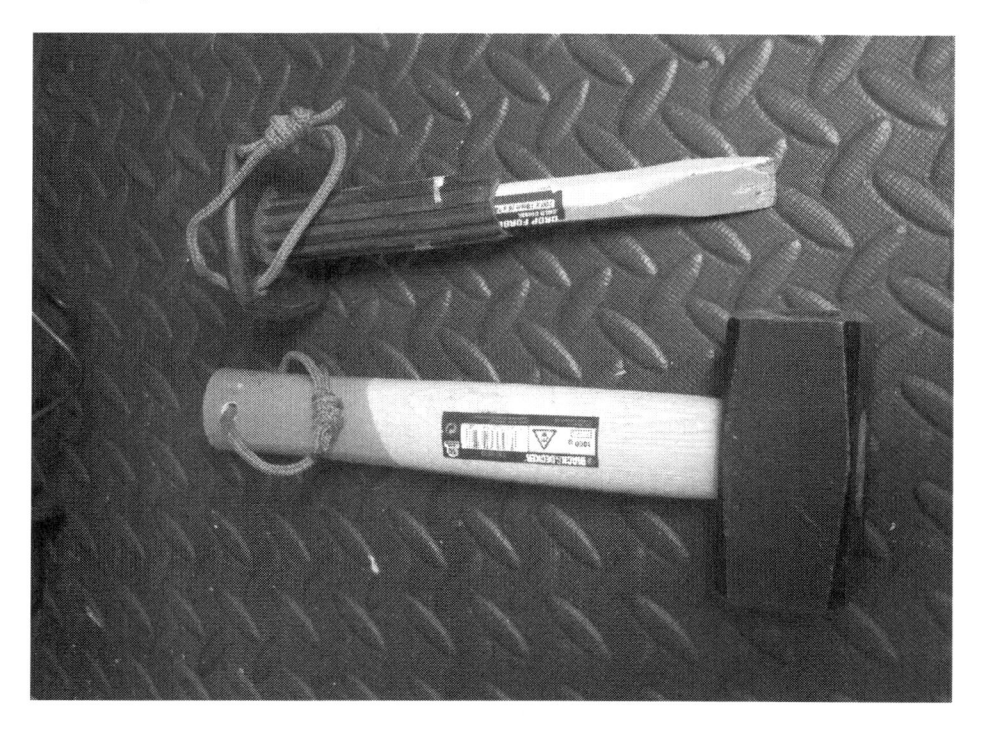

That completed and the samples numbered and put away in the relevant barrel, I made a cup of coffee and while boiling the water put the mouth piece from my water bottle into it to wash out. While drinking the coffee outside, I walked about looking for sections of the faces where I might be able to get down on ropes easily in order to collect further rock samples and take magnetic variation measurements. I think I will be able to get down most of the faces bar two, the main East face, which it's just not worth abseiling down on my own due to the exposure, and part of the South West face, which is fairly featureless and slightly overhanging. I may, however, be able to get into the latter partially, at either side, from the adjacent facets of the same face.

While thinking about that, it occurred to me that in addition to a pen, note book, camera and compass, I would also have to take a hammer and chisel down with me and wouldn't have the pockets to fit all this equipment in. So, I then drilled holes in the wooden handle of the lump hammer and into the rubber flange at the top of the grip on the chisel so that I could thread paracord through them and clip them to the gear loops on my climbing harness, thus keeping my hands free to climb. It took a little while as I only have masonry drill bits with me, which don't go through wood very quickly. Finally, I went around the stainless steel pulleys, now that I'm happy with their locations, and tightened up the shackles attaching the pulleys to the rock fixings, which were only finger tight, with my Leatherman in preparation for wiring them to prevent them coming undone.

A couple of times this morning I noticed a stench of rotting meat in the air, which I have not smelt before. It's not like the constant smell of dead fish on the rock, which I have become used to and now don't really notice. There were no fishing boats in the direction the wind was coming from, so I'm working on the assumption that there's something dead and floating to the East of me at the moment. It can't, however, be too close as I would expect birds to be all over a whale carcass for example, and I couldn't see any massing. Nor was it a constant smell, indicating that the source was nearby. I'll keep a look out. Before lunch, I did my exercises with the Thera-band, which I'm currently trying to do every other day, when I remember.

In the afternoon I was feeling cold and had achy guts, which soon manifested as a bad stomach. I therefore rested for the rest of the day until early evening, listening to music on my iPod and reading for a while. Having finished the last autobiography I was on, I've now moved to something slightly more academic and am working my way through a recently transcribed document recounting an archaeological tour of the Mediterranean in 1811 and 1812, coincidentally around the time Basil Hall first landed here, for my friend Mike, who is a Professor of Ancient History in Sicily, in order to let him know how it reads and what changes to the format I would suggest. The sun came out later on, and I was feeling a little better, so I put the hammer and chisel away in their barrel, and looked for possible transect lines on which to take the magnetic deviation measurements for St. Andrew's.

By the evening, the wind had turned to the south and was picking up slowly from being near still earlier in the day. This was forecast and was the start of a continual building of wind speed over the next thirty six hours up to the forecasted peak early on Wednesday morning.

Forecast from WindGuru (http://www.windguru.cz)

While playing around with my radio again tonight, I finally managed to get the BBC World Service on Shortwave, having previously only managed to find Spanish, French and Chinese stations. Typically though, I tuned in just as a half hour programme on the football World Cup was starting, and as one of the reasons I'm glad I landed on Rockall this year was that I was going to miss the blanket coverage, I switched it off for another day. However, my spirits were lifted when I realised that tomorrow will be the first of July, which means that when I wake tomorrow I'll be heading home next month, and by enjoying the pleasant evening before settling in.

Day 27 – 1st July

It's the first of July today, which means I've been here for most of June and I'll be heading back to normality next month! I woke early, around 0630. I'm not sure why, but the wind was up so it could have been that or the latrine bucket hitting the side of the pod, which I'll move behind the pod later today. However, I was able to turn over and dozed until around 0840. I was surprised to see that it was a clear blue sky, even though the wind was already around twenty to twenty five miles per hour, and was in fact pleasant and mild, save for the wind chill. I completed my normal morning rituals and then read more of Mike's paper for an hour or so.

I've been wondering what the birds will do in the high winds, whether they will abandon Rockall for the sea, or if they'll move into the lee of the rock. Currently, the guillemots which are not the most efficient on the wing, are generally settled on the rock, with the gulls and kittiwakes gliding overhead using the speed of the wind for elevation and not wasting any energy flapping their wings. The heavier gannets are still having to fly, although appear on the verge of being able to glide too. It will be interesting to monitor how their techniques develop as the wind speed rises through the day.

With the wind rising, but it being warmer than usual (excluding the wind chill) at almost sixteen degrees centigrade, I was able to spend much of the morning standing in the pod with my top half out, warm jacket on, Buff around my neck and a hat on, watching the waves and birds, and enjoying that feeling that strong wind can give you of being alive. By two in the afternoon, it was gusting towards thirty miles per hour and so I retreated to the RockPod, closed the hatch and read. When I did emerge to pee, I noticed that one of the kittiwakes had red rings on its legs. This is the first ringed bird that's not a pigeon I've seen here. If I can, I'll attempt to record any markings on the rings, but I think that will be unlikely in these conditions.

I got a bit bored of reading and stiff from lying down for so long this morning, but because of the wind I couldn't really sit up straight without fully opening the top hatch on the pod, which I didn't want to do in case it got caught by the wind and blown back. I managed to fashion a restraint by using the loops of paracord around the handle I use to get in the RockPod, and tying overhand knots in them to provide a shorter leash which I could loop over the hook on the hatch handles, thereby allowing it to be open enough for me to sit upright and peer out. It was interesting that there were still at least two boats out trawling in this weather, particularly with gales forecast, but I know little about trawling and perhaps they had not caught enough fish yet to warrant an early return to port.

Shortly after three o'clock I decided I needed to pee so stood up out of the hatch as usual. The fates conspired that at exactly that moment, the first wave to hit Rockall and spray Hall's Ledge since I arrived here hit me. It got me squarely on my right hand side and went in through the wide open hatch. Fortunately I seem to have taken the brunt of the water with a small pool on the floor inside the pod, some minor splashing to the wall and water cans, and a tiny amount of ricochet spray on the charge controller. I was both unfortunate, in my timing, and lucky that more kit and electrics did not get soaked. I quickly mopped up the worst of the water in the pod with sponges and towelled dried the floor, which although foam rubber doesn't seem to soak up the water too much.

The problem now is that, even rung out, the towel and sponges won't dry fully because the salt in the sea water will attract moisture, and my warm clothes are now damp too. It also means that I can't really risk having the top hatch open for the rest of the day, which is a pain, literally in my back. The hatch is now only open to the ventilation level, which I think should be ok as the hatch overhangs the frame and its moulding is designed to divert water away from the opening; but until I witness water actually landing on it, I'll need to keep all my electronics away from that end of the pod. The reason I'm not closing it fully immediately is that even with the deck vent open, condensation tends to build up on the glass of the top hatch if it's fully locked down and drip onto me and the floor! I'll also have to now start using a pee bottle. My other problem, with the hatches being almost fully closed, is that the temperature inside the pod went up to twenty six degrees centigrade, so I had to strip down to my underwear in order not to overheat.

I spent the rest of the day in the pod, finishing reading the historical document and watching the sea state outside. It was good to note that the forecast from Windguru was very accurate in regards to timings and corresponded with the information that my weather station on Rockall's summit was feeding me about the actual conditions.

Day 28 – 2nd July

The second of July 2014 will go down as the date I was last properly scared. I got no sleep at all last night. The wind continued to build and the RockPod was regularly hit by not just spray but also hard green water. I tried to doze through it with my ear plugs in, and was quite successful until around 0300 when a loud thump hit the pod and it moved! I'm not certain how far we were shunted across Hall's Ledge; maybe an inch maybe a foot, but I then felt the pod skid back to near its original position. Immediately I thought about breaking the promise I'd made to my wife; about not making it home safely. You learn very quickly what's important in your life as you wait in silence to be swept off the only solid object in a tempestuous ocean, unable to do a single thing about it.

I was frightened, and was not able to go outside due to the conditions. I had to hope that all the ratchet straps were still intact and attached. I wished I'd stretched the expedition budget to ones with clips rather than just hooks on the ends as they wouldn't have unhooked if the straps became very slack. I just had to lie there and wait. I thought about how this would be a different night if either the wind or waves had been from another direction, instead of both heralding from the south, and compounding each other's effect on my southerly facing perch.

I spent most of the rest of the night in the foetal position, literally jumping every time spray or water hit the pod, and being dripped on constantly from a combination of condensation build up inside the pod, as I had all the hatches tightly closed, and from a small leak at the hinge of the main hatch above me, which I thought I'd sealed previously but apparently not. Closing the hatches had also caused the temperature within the pod to increase to twenty eight degrees centigrade; I couldn't tell the outside temperature as there was no reading on the weather station base unit, so I had to assume that the weather station on the summit has been lost to the storm.

I'd had to close both the hatches as soon as the waves started to hit the ledge and the pod in order to prevent the impact pressure forcing water into the RockPod and swamping all my kit and supplies. I had fitted a deck vent for specifically this scenario, but that too started to allow water in when hit by direct deluges. I therefore closed that too, re-opening it when I could to allow some transfer of air for me to breathe. Adding to the issue of my own body heat raising the temperature inside the pod was the fact that the high winds meant that the turbine had rapidly recharged the battery and the charge controller was then dumping all the excess and constant charge as heat into the shelter's interior. With the hatches and vent shut tight down, there was nowhere for the heat to escape. Perhaps I hadn't needed to insulate the pod so well after all. I thought, albeit too late, that tying off the turbine blades would have prevented this, but I hadn't wanted to risk the high winds damaging the turbine for future use if the blades weren't able to spin at all.

At first light, and timing my exit until after waves had sprayed down the pod, I popped my head out of the RockPod to check that all the ratchet straps were still in place, which thankfully they were. There was also a huge amount of seaweed on the deck of the pod, testament to the height that the waves had reached in the night. Once the sun was up and the wind had died a little, I could check properly and saw that at least three of the straps at the East end of the pod were loose. More disappointing was the fact that several of my kit barrels, and my latrine bucket, were missing. There seemed to be a short lull in the weather so I dashed out when I could, tightened the ratchet straps and accounted for a total of four barrels missing. I was lucky that the slack in the ratchet straps hadn't led to me losing one or more of them by their becoming unhooked; in hindsight I really should have obtained ones with spring-loaded clips on the ends instead of the normal open hooks, which would have removed any chance of them becoming unattached.

In addition, the back-up solar panels were disconnected from their leash and had jammed under the ground anchor end of a ratchet strap at the very edge of Hall's Ledge just before the cliff edge. I retrieved the panels, putting them behind the pod, and moved the remaining barrels to safer locations. Once audited, I confirmed that I had lost one large barrel containing my buoyancy aid and climbing hardware (but not the ropes), and three smaller barrels, numbers three, five and six, which contained amongst other things, rations, my waterproof jacket which I hadn't been using, and spare pieces of kit and equipment. I had also lost my life-line which I used whenever I left the safety of the pod and moved around the rock, attached to my climbing harness. I'd habitually left it clipped to the outside of the shelter whenever I got back in so that it was to hand each time I climbed back out through the top hatch. I think I was lucky not to lose more.

Depressed, I returned to the pod to think over my options and calculate how many days' rations I had left. Once back inside, I noticed a large crack in the ceiling of the pod, across the insulation. I could not be certain whether this was due to the foam shrinking in the hot internal environment the night before, or due to the impact of water hitting this point outside. It will in either case serve as a permanent reminder, if I needed it, of what happened that night. I decided I needed to know the forecast for the next couple of weeks; the weather is forecast to improve over the next week, but I don't think I would be able to mentally weather another storm like last night, nor did I know what unseen damage had been done to the pod.

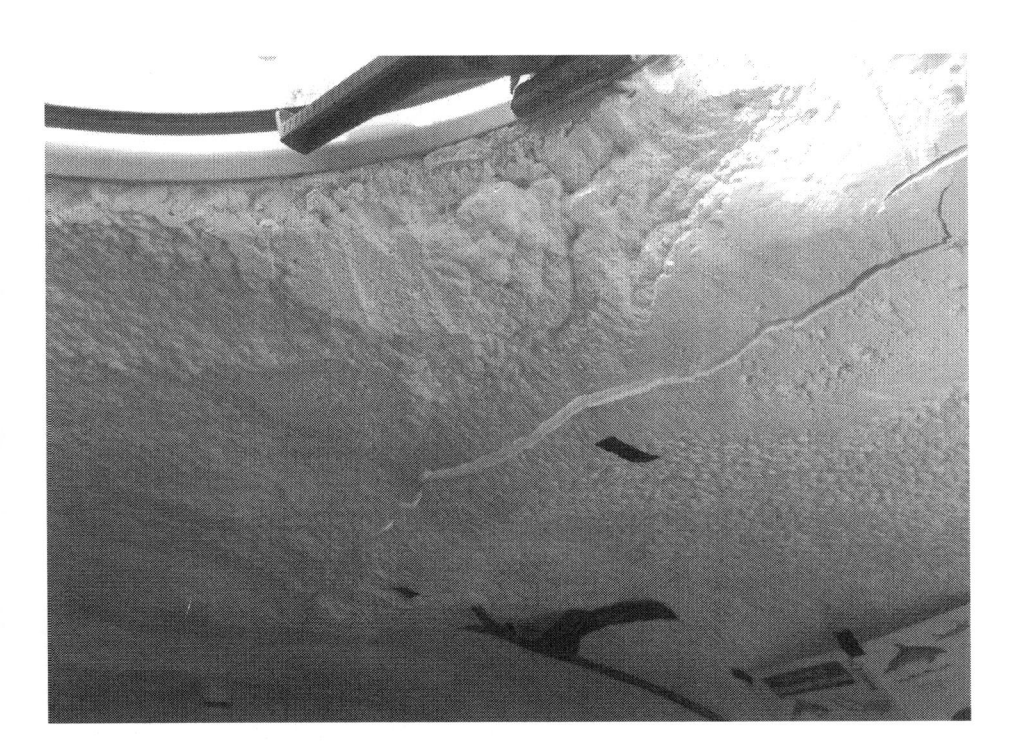

I managed to go online and confirm the improving picture for the next seven days, and I had calculated that I had enough rations to still go for the occupation records if the weather holds. Feeling more positive, I called my wife on my Isatphone2 to tell her the news and my plans, which were to call both Angus Smith and Angus Campbell to update them, try and obtain a long range forecast, and explore my options for shortening the expedition; call Iain McIver, my press officer, to update him (he in fact contacted Angus Smith on my behalf) and my wife also suggested that I call HM Coastguard Stornoway just to update them of my situation and outline intentions. I thought they may also have a long range forecast, which they did not. Then I had a cup of tea.

Randomly, just after breakfast, a dump of water on the pod came through the closed top hatch and resulted in a pool on the floor again. I quickly soaked this up with sponges and squeezed them through the side window. I couldn't see anything wrong with the seals on the hatch, so have to put it down to a freakishly accurate wave and perhaps a not fully closed hatch. Iain rang me back around midday to say he'd spoken to Angus Smith, a very experienced open ocean skipper, who confirmed that the weather was improving, and changing direction in my favour. He also said that he couldn't see any weather for the next two weeks that should cause me a serious problem, which is great news although obviously the accuracy of forecasts drops away with time.

I called my wife back to tell her about the weather forecast and also to placate her worrying a bit by letting her know that I'd fashioned a new lifeline from a redundant short lifting strop and a couple of karabiners I still had. The temperature in the pod had by that point reached thirty degrees, and shortly after topped thirty one. I decided that I really had to vent the pod somehow, so placed an already soaked towel in the partially open ventilation gap of the main top hatch in order to catch any water, and then opened the South facing side hatch ajar too as the wind was now driving the spray from the West.

Much of the rest of the day was spent lying looking out of the top hatch, listening to the wind, waiting for the waves to spray the pod and wishing it would all calm down, or at least the wind would stop. Around 1800 I called Angus Campbell, who was just back from St. Kilda. He had heard some of my predicament, and we discussed where I was at: I still had all my water and enough rations to get me through to at least the 17th, which was the day after the solo record. I told him that it was my preferred option to stay until then, but that I would need to come off the rock soon after as I had no more food – he suggested fishing, but I did not want to have to rely on that, particularly as it would mean being outside on the edge of the cliff in poor weather. My confidence was truly shot.

Angus said that he would look at his diary, but he knew that he was fully booked with day trips to St. Kilda until my proposed sixty day mark; he would see if he could clear anything and at the same time ask around for any other vessels that might come for me. We agreed to speak again tomorrow, but within the hour he called me back to say that as there was good weather at the start of next week, he could move his passengers from the end of the week to there, which would give him four days at the end of that week, assuming good weather, in which he could come for me. This was before the dates of the records, but I had to take the view that it was better to take the opportunity to come off safely, before my food ran out, than beat the records and have no option but to call out the Coastguard and abandon all my kit and the pod on Rockall. That being agreed, I called my wife and Iain McIver to let them know. Iain had already sent out a press release earlier in the day, and Pam told me that it had been on the news that I had lost kit.

Feeling more positive as I had a new goal to aim for, but at the same time disappointed I'd miss the records by just a few days, even though I knew it was the right thing to do, I attempted to eat something as I was not feeling great and had not eaten much through the day. Around 2000 I felt very tired, having not slept the night before and resolved to try and sleep early. Still worried about the weather and with my mind racing about the possibility of more gales, I quickly put on my dry suit with my harness and new lifeline and settled in. I even thought about what I wanted to and could take with me in the event of needing to be rescued. I put my hard drive, with all the expedition photos, videos and diary from the expedition, and a small book (Omar Khyam which my Grandfather had given me) in a waterproof box which fitted in one of the trouser pockets of my dry suit, and I planned to take my Grandfather's binoculars around my neck beneath the dry suit. Everything else would have to be abandoned. Surprisingly, I fell asleep quite quickly and slept well, waking every few hours when I became stiff or uncomfortable, changing positions and falling asleep again.

Day 29 – 3rd July

I finally awoke around 0800 and dozed until 0830, feeling rested and more clear headed. I set off my SPOT Messenger as usual and tried to think about what I should do with my day. Briefly, I rang my wife to let her know all was ok and promised to speak to her later in the day. I then went about restoring some order to the inside of the pod, mopping up traces of water and getting out of my dry suit. I was quite damp inside the suit, I assumed from sweating during the night, which was backed up by the colour of my urine when I first peed into the bottle this morning. When I removed my socks, quite a bit of skin came off with them, and there was a definite pong about the pod. Having not washed for a month, I think this is just an accumulation of dead skin which has come off with the damp.

After breakfast, I spent much of the first half of the morning pondering and listening, waiting for the forecasted drop in the wind and slow decrease in wave height. A call came in over the Isatphone2 from The Times, and I spoke briefly to a reporter there, before continuing with my thoughts and putting the phone on to charge. I wanted to go online to get an up to date forecast, and also wanted to get any vital kit and rations out of the barrels, but daren't yet due to the waves still splashing the RockPod, and the fact that a lull was forecast at the end of the day.

I had also had a text on the satellite phone this morning from one of my sponsors, LPG Exceptional Energy, asking if they could get more food out to me and offering to seek sponsorship to pay for it. Having already decided on and being focussed for coming off next week, I still felt that I had to consider this offer. Giving it serious thought, I reminded myself that I didn't feel psychologically ready to go through another storm like that on the 2nd, and there may be another ahead which would cause me serious issues; the pod may have unseen damage and could be damaged further, and I couldn't afford to lose more kit barrels. In addition, the cost of getting the food to me was likely to run into thousands of pounds, which I seriously felt would be better going straight to the charity at this point. It was only then, with this option given to me, that I accepted that the weather had beaten me and that it was time to go home.

Once the phone was charged I brought it back up to the head end of the pod where I got a good signal inside and immediately got a call from my wife saying that Iain had been trying to contact me as NBC wanted to do a live Skype interview across America. I immediately called him and explained that I couldn't Skype as I didn't want to have the top hatch open but that I could speak to them over the phone. NBC called me back within ten minutes and put me through to the live studio; unfortunately although I could hear them, they could not hear me and so there was no interview, but the piece Rupert had edited, and for which I'd previously uploaded the videos, had been broadcast, which was great news.

I called my wife back to tell her what had happened and also because it occurred to me that she would be sat in front of her computer at work and so could get me an up to date forecast. As I half expected, the Windguru forecast had changed and the wind and waves were not altering direction as early as previously forecast, which explained why I was still getting sprayed, and worse still the Met Office had issued a new gale warning for the Rockall area, Force 8. Resigned to more bad weather, I settled in for the afternoon, and started reading 'The Long Walk to Freedom' by Nelson Mandela. I noticed that some birds had returned, and took this as a good omen of improving weather as they were looking to rest on the rock.

Around 1415, the wind suddenly dropped outside and when I looked at the turbine it had moved to the North West, so that I was now sheltered from what was obviously still a strong wind by the back wall of the rock. This was followed at 1435 by rain, but I was glad of some respite and less noise from the wind. The waves also seemed to have dropped when I next put my head out of the hatch, and I caught myself breathing an involuntary sigh of relief. The rest of the afternoon was spent reading and resting. It started raining again around 1800 and shortly after, the wind turbine stopped! No wind!

I spoke again to Angus Campbell this afternoon, who said that having consulted with Angus Smith, the weather did not look great for them coming out next week and should be better the week after. There were also two new boats coming available which could cover Kilda Cruises' other commitments, and so he felt certain that they could come and get me off Rockall just after the records, which was actually great news at it gives this whole recent episode some purpose after all. While letting my wife know over the Isatphone, I actually welled up and had a lump in my throat when I was speaking to her again about the storm, a sign of how much it has actually affected me, which surprised me a lot. My fragile mental state was not helped either when my little boy Freddie asked, "You coming home to me?".

After my first hot meal for a couple of days, as I was either too tired to cook or was too busy doing other admin, I heard squawking outside and managed to watch the newly returned and bedraggled kittiwakes for a few minutes, despite the rain, and was pleased to see them back. Once I settled in for the night, my jerry-rigged sponge drip catchers started to leak and I was getting a wet head. Thinking about the issue, I realised that in the absence of any silicone sealant, which if I had I wouldn't have been trying to use in this weather anyway, an elongated rubber seal around the screw holes should do the trick. I didn't have one, but reasoned that a doubled over elastic band might work. Using my Leatherman, I quickly opened the top hatch and partially unscrewed the hinge. Lifting the external plate to which the hinge attaches, I looped the band around the plastic lugs that pass through the glass of the hatch to the hinge. Screwing everything tight again, it seemed to do the trick, or at least restricted the flow of the leak, which I was happy with.

Day 30 – 4th July

Today had been a massive milestone for over a week as it marked the half way point to the end of the sixty day challenge, and psychologically everything would be downhill from here, counting down the days until I returned home. However, after the events of the past week, it is now significantly less than a month until I plan to head home, and so I was simply pleased to have been here for a month.

I woke initially around 0630 but dozed until around 0800 when the wind, which had picked up again, meant that I was properly awake. I had an early and quite a quick breakfast, as it was forecast to rain again later and I wanted to get out of the pod, properly go through the remaining barrels and sort out the safety ropes, which had been partially washed down the cliffs, and tie up the loose ends of the ratchet straps which were flapping in the wind and hitting the pod.

First of all, I took out a large bag of rubbish, and put it in the rubbish barrel, which typically the sea gods had seen fit to leave me, and put the damp and stinking socks into another barrel. I then went to the East end of the pod, hauled up the safety rope there and coiled it neatly, and tidied up the ratchet straps, checking their tension as I went.

I was able to see from the position of the strap in the groove running over the deck of the RockPod that the pod was now about two inches further west than it had originally been. As it had returned to this position after moving further, we must have been shoved almost half a foot! To my great surprise, I also saw the tail end of my life line sticking out from under the pod and was able to retrieve this, with no apparent damage, and am now using it again. While at this end of the pod, I saw that the whole weather station is still there on the summit, but being bent over at ninety degrees and with the battery compartment having probably been swamped; there is still no signal from it. I may go up and have a closer look if the wind drops.

Moving to the West end of the pod, I checked the tension in the wind turbine guy wire as I passed, which was fine, and coiled up the safety rope at that end of the pod too, again with no apparent damage. Both the patio and the redundant light housing had been scrubbed clean of guano, testament to the power of the water that hit here, and as the 'seat' area was now clear, due to the loss of barrels and me moving the remainder to behind the pod, I could see that fortunately I had not lost the board for covering and protecting the glass top hatch when the pod is lowered from the rock, which was jammed beneath the pod.

Next I moved to the residual barrels, moving systematically through them, taking out the remaining rations, putting them in the pod, and checking what other kit I had left. I was pleased to see that all the loaned tools were still here (drill, resin gun, etc.) along with the two small bottles of champagne I brought to celebrate the records, the Help for Heroes banner, which I shall re-erect at some point, and the bottle of Abhainn-Dearg whisky. Even though it was 'officially' a day early, I also treated myself to a clean pair of underwear and socks and, while it was dry, I spent a few minutes just standing by the pod before going back in to try and re-adjust myself to the environment, and to enjoy being able to stand up properly after two or three days of lying and sitting only.

Back in the pod, I tidied up the kit I had brought in from the barrels and counted up my days' rations. I still had fifty days' worth of food, which confirms my initial appraisal of not being able to reach the sixty day mark, but it does give me some leeway should weather prevent Kilda Cruises coming for me as planned. Having slept on it, I'm convinced that going back shortly after the two records is still the right decision, importantly for me mentally, but also because of the risk of the possibility of very bad weather again. The sixty day idea was always just an ideal goal, a nice round two months which would push the records out significantly, hopefully beyond the reach of anyone for a while. I am not disappointed that I will not reach sixty days, but I would have been had I been forced to abandon Rockall before achieving the occupation records.

I read more all afternoon, not wanting to go out into the wind and deeply wishing it would stop. There's a calm day forecast tomorrow before higher winds again on Sunday, so I'm hoping I can settle my nerves over the next twenty four hours or so. It's strange, as I know I'm not in danger, I might get a bit of spray on the pod, but there seems to be this deep dread in me now that I can't shake.

Day 31 – 5th July

I woke to a lovely day, as forecast, with the wind from the North West so that I was sheltered behind the summit. I slept fairly well considering, and woke about 0800. I had a slow breakfast, with the top hatch wide open for a change as it was sunny and warm. I'm trying to force myself back into my old routine, so took a while over breakfast, even though I finished much earlier than I would have previously, due to when I woke up. It was fun to see the first few black-headed gulls since I've been here. It just goes to show that I probably won't have seen everything that happens out at Rockall even in my time here.

As it was such a nice morning, and would potentially rain later on, I resolved to get out of the RockPod and move around the rock for a while in order to get used to it again. I took my camera, and got photos of where the rock had been scrubbed clean of guano by the waves, the location of a large gannet nest with egg just down from the summit, which had disappeared, the new position of the ratchet straps over the top of the pod, and various other bits and pieces. I also noted that the light housing on the summit was flooded after the storm, which would suggest that any eggs the Guillemots lay in there are unlikely to ever hatch.

I checked the barrels again, and had a brief look inside them so that I could gauge whether I have enough room to pack away all the kit that is inside the pod when I leave, which I think I do. I then went up to the summit and repositioned the weather station, which was still leaning over after being battered in the storm, in the hope that it might start recording again, although the battery compartment was fairly wet inside, so I doubt it. Next were some exercises, which included squats on the patio and calf raises on the seat at the West of the ledge. Shortly afterwards I heard a howling noise, and looking over the edge I saw two seals in the lee of the waves calling to each other. I'm not sure what they were doing, but it was a new noise for me out here, which was novel; the minke also reappeared around the same time.

Finally, I had a think about where I could lower the pod down when I leave. The original plan was just to drop it down the cliff, where I had winched it up, using a friction device called a Petzl ID; but as I'd lost both the IDs I'd brought with me in the storm I now have to come up with a new plan. There is always the option of just pushing the pod off the cliff and hoping for the best, but this would be a last resort as there is a chance that the hatches may break with the impact, and if the pod rolled it would fill with water and be lost.

I want to take the RockPod home as it is by far the most iconic symbol of the expedition, and someone may like it for a maritime museum one day. I decided that probably the best option would be to try and lower it down the south facing slope at the side of the East end of Hall's Ledge. I thought I could turn the pod ninety degrees so it would go down nose first, and as the majority of the terrain was sloped, I hoped that the friction between the rock and the pod would aid me in lowering it. There is still be a drop at the end, but it is about quarter of the height of the East cliff, and I am confident that the pod would easily survive the impact from this height. Time will tell.

I continued my exercises with the Thera-band inside the pod, and then read with the hatch open, enjoying the still air and blue skies, until 1400 when the heavens opened and there was a heavy downpour. Afterwards, and I'm assuming because the rock is cleaner, there wasn't the usual smell of rotten fish when the rock is wet, just a musty whiff as it dried in the sun.

I've had a couple of random drips of water appear inside the pod today when it hasn't been raining. I can't work out exactly why, but am putting it down to water or condensation trapped between the internal insulation layer of foam and the plastic shell of the pod, expanding in the increased heat and working its way out. It was also good to see a couple of trawlers back, one of which was familiar: PD340 Ocean Venture. Seeing them felt like confirmation of improved weather for a sustained period. This evening I've re-read the instructions from Tim Raub of St. Andrew's University in regard to the rock sampling, geo-magnetism and orientation surveys he's asked me to undertake, as I hope to commence those next week. My flabby brain, from a month of not being used much, took three or four readings before I thought I understood what he was asking me to do!

I'll read it again in the morning.

Day 32 – 6th July

Again I woke up early, around 0730, but managed to doze until just after 0800. I was not pleased as it had taken me a while to get to sleep last night, last time I checked my watch it was after midnight, so I was tired and it also meant that I had more hours to fill today. As forecast, the wind was up, but from the North West so I was fairly sheltered from it. The waves were rougher too, and I could hear them breaking around the other side of the rock. It was also drizzling, and while I had breakfast, listening to some music, the rain came and went.

I read all morning, having a coffee around 1100, as with the increased wind and cloud cover it was a lot cooler today, before the sun came out and I could watch the trawlers for a while. Interestingly the same drips as yesterday appeared as soon as the sun emerged, so I'm fairly certain they've got something to do with water expanding somewhere. This may mean that the weight of the pod has increased due to water ingress. I am also concerned about the area beneath the floor where spray got in, as it may create difficulties for me moving the pod on my own when I come to leave.

Also while reading, shortly before lunch, I felt something on my hand and looked down to see an insect crawling across it. I immediately went for the tweezers in my invertebrate collection kit, and on closer inspection it appeared to be a tick. The tick went into alcohol along with the other invertebrates I've gathered, and I wondered if it had been brought here by birds and somehow worked its way into the pod. Another source may be that I have a number of items of my hill walking clothing with me, and perhaps tick eggs had somehow survived the clothes being washed and recently hatched. I resolved to keep an eye out for further invaders![26]

As forecast, the weather did not improve in the afternoon, and in fact turned a little windier and wilder. Just before 1600 a wave splashed heavily over the pod; fortunately I had closed the top hatch with the expectation of rain. Its suddenness made me jump and my heart raced for a short while. I realised

---

[26] Appendix A

that although yesterday had been calming and raised my spirits, I was still not fully over the storm of earlier in the week. I took solace in the forecast saying that 1600 was the peak of the wind and waves for the next three days at least.

The wind meant that I continued to read for the remainder of the afternoon, finishing Nelson Mandela's autobiography and making a start on that of Malcolm X. Just before bedtime I noticed that my left eye was producing some gunk. I'd always expected to get an eye infection here, even with watching my hygiene, as you always subconsciously rub your eyes during the day and also I've been wearing an eye mask each night to sleep, which is getting a bit dirty. The eye wasn't too red, but I thought I should nip any infection in the bud and so started a course of Chloramphenicol eye ointment from my medical kit.

Day 33 – 7th July

It's only one week until the solo record today, and I was glad to wake up a little later this morning, to a Fresh Breeze and blue skies with some cloud. My eye seemed alright, and not as gunky as last night, but I continued with the treatment never the less. As I had not been able to check the forecast last night due to the wind and rain, I made a cup of tea and then went online via the Inmarsat BGAN unit and checked the forecast. It looks really good for the rest of the week, with decreasing winds and seas throughout the week which gives me hope of a settled end to the expedition. I'd really like to get back to the point I was at before the storm before I leave, when I was enjoying being here and considering it a privilege.

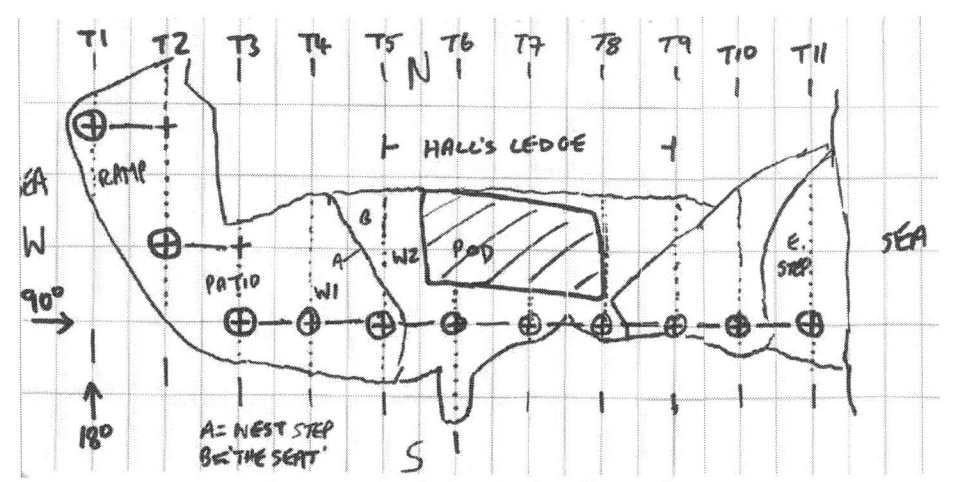

Extract from notebook showing baseline and transects

Over a cup of coffee after breakfast, I tried to think about the best way to get the most and longest transects for the geomagnetism survey, within the restrictions of my newly confined movements brought about by the loss of my climbing hardware in the storm. I set up a baseline, running on a bearing of ninety degrees, along the edge of Hall's Ledge. I then looked to see where on that line I could place a central transect that would extend the furthest South from it. From there I marked every one metre along the baseline. As the baseline did not extend all the way from the edge of The Ramp to the edge of the East Step, I also had to set up two off-set baselines to accommodate these extra areas. I then set up transects from these points, eleven in total, on a bearing of eighteen degrees, which was the bearing along the transect line extending the furthest South. This grid gave me the maximum coverage of the flattest area of Rockall.

Next I had to measure any magnetic deflection caused by the rock. Every twenty five centimetres along each transect line, above and below the baseline where possible, I would check that my compass was showing the correct bearing along the transect about a metre above the rock. Then lowering the compass to the rock at the marked intervals, I would record any deflection in the bearing at rock level. I continue in this way all morning and completed six of the eleven transects before lunch, when I retired to the RockPod as I was getting cold from being in the North Westerly wind at the western end of the ledge, and wanted to eat. While having lunch I wrote some notes about my survey and added some detail to the sketches I'd drawn while taking the measurements, in the hope that they would help whoever's processing the data to understand it better.

While taking these measurements I passed very close to the Collinox fixing I had placed in The Patio, which I had worried was loaded ninety degrees in the wrong direction before the storm. I had not been able to correct it as the resin set very quickly, but hoped it would hold. It did hold, but very close inspection today showed that the fixing was actually now slightly bent in towards the RockPod in the direction of the ratchet straps at the other end of the pod that had become slack after the storm. This awakened a renewed feeling of dread in my stomach, and I'm very glad that it held; there is a lesson in there regarding placing fixings! While having lunch I watched a couple of minke whales, a long tailed skua, and few puffins pass by. My VHF radio had started to buzz every now and again last night, to the point that I had to turn it down as it became annoying; it continued today over lunch as well. I suppose that there may be a fault on one of the trawlers radios which is accidentally causing it to transmit every now and again.

I continued reading for much of the afternoon, interspersed with exercising and renaming some of the photos I've taken while doing this morning's survey, so that they make more sense to whoever's using them for reference. This evening I went online to check emails, get some weather updates, and arrange an interview for tomorrow lunchtime with another US TV network. I was a bit worried to see a forecast for a week today of high winds, gusting over forty miles per hour. I double checked with my wife who gets the same forecast in a different format, and hers showed very low winds for the same period, so I'm not sure which to believe nor why there's a difference in the same forecast. I'm hoping hers is correct and will check again tomorrow when I go online for the interview.

Day 34 – 8th July

I slept fitfully again, waking several times in the night for no apparent reason, and then finally getting up around 0800 having dozed for as long as I could. It was a clear day, blue skies, with a stiff breeze from which I was sheltered. The forecast was for it to get calmer during the day although there would be more cloud cover later on. As usual, I took things slowly and ended up not having breakfast until almost 0930. I decided to read for most of the morning, until my interview, and then planned to continue with the survey this afternoon.

Reproduced with permission Simon Wright

Around 1045, I looked up to see a large white shape on the Western horizon. Looking through the binoculars it looked to be a big ship, heading roughly towards Rockall, with a reddish hull. Even from that distance, it was obviously much bigger than anything else I've seen since I got here. Around an hour later they were close enough for me to see, through the binoculars, that the ship was called the 'James Clark Ross', a research vessel. I called them up on the VHF and chatted to a lady for about ten minutes about the expedition, waving for them to take photos as they went past. They had come from Canada, and were on their way up to Iceland, but were stopping about one and a half miles away to carry out some research here, before moving on. Apparently they will be returning to Rockall in a few days too, so that will mean a familiar 'face' to look forward to then.

After a while, they obviously finished whatever they were doing and came back on the radio to say that they were going to come close past the rock. They came within a couple of hundred metres, and it was great to see such a big ship so close. I took lots of photos and video, shouted across to them, they responded, and I counted over thirty people looking at me through the binoculars. Nothing happens for ages then typically, this was all just around 1300 and coincided with when I had an interview booked with Inside Edition. Luckily they called around 1315, and so I was able to talk to them for around twenty minutes, and relate the story of the ship coming so close. Shortly afterwards, I notice three bonxies hovering over the summit of Rockall, which is not great news. I'm hoping they don't see me as a source of food, as I know from experience that they can be very aggressive and will dive-bomb people, causing head injuries. Hopefully they'll move on or away soon, but in the meantime I partially closed the top hatch on the pod as a precaution. I also seem to have developed a twitch under my right eye today, which is annoying, but doesn't visibly seem to have any external cause. I'm hoping it will pass soon too.

After lunch I read for a while, then while looking in one of the kit barrels I realised that I hadn't put my Help for Heroes banner back up on the rock face after the storm, which was a shame as it would have been picked up in the pictures the crew of the James Clark Ross took today. I went out to put it up, and while out thought that I might as well practice taking rock samples, with strike and dip angle measurements, for St. Andrew's. Needless to say, once I started I got into it and ended up collecting several good samples. Unfortunately, a number pirouetted down the cliff and into the sea as my attempts to stop them doing so failed and they bounced past my feet and legs. I also finished off yesterday's exercise session with squats and calf raises on the West step and patio, before getting thirsty and heading back inside to read for the remainder of the afternoon. The bonxies didn't hang about for too long, thankfully, but I did notice that a large group of gannets arrived and seemed to be landing on the North side of rock, which may be why the bonxies are about, as they parasitically pester other birds until they drop their catch and the skuas then swoop in and claim it.

Day 35 – 9th July

I managed to sleep better and a little longer last night, and didn't wake up until 0830. The weather was dull, with a close fog at around one hundred metres, which restricted visibility, a southerly breeze, and drizzle. Before breakfast I ran a diagnostic tool on the BGAN unit as I have been having some issues with the unit recognising the batteries and booting up, and the support team need the reports for both, which I will email to them later today. The problem is, I think, one of manufacturing as I received a short instructional video from them the other day describing how to scrape the green insulation off the electronic board that makes up the battery terminal, as apparently it is too thick and is restricting the contacts.

After breakfast I was in the mood for some Italian, and so proceeded through several lessons on the Ergo laptop for around an hour, which I enjoyed. I have not completed as many lessons in Italian or on the harmonica as I would have liked, but I've found that I really have to be in the mood to do it in order to be motivated, and I have preferred to read more than anything else whilst here. Nice to have a choice of things to do though. After that, the weather had cleared up a bit, visibility was back to normal, it was drier and the wind had moved around to the south west. Shortly after I looked out and saw a group of six terns being followed by a skua up high; one of the terns had obviously had enough and was pestering the bonxie in the hope that it would leave them alone.

I then read for most of the rest of the morning and into the early afternoon as two or three separate fog banks rolled past from the West. Each time one passed, the wind speed picked up and the air was noticeably more moist, depositing dew onto the RockPod and the top hatch if I'd left it open for a little too long. In between bouts of reading I practice tying a 'super munter hitch' on a piece of paracord. I knew about and have used basic munter hitches before I came to Rockall; a munter or alpine hitch is basically a hitch onto a karabiner which imparts friction to a rope by the rope exerting pressure on itself, so that the rope can still move through the karabiner but the friction restricts that movement, allowing you to lower a heavy object or person slowly and under control.

The so-called 'super munter' had been suggested to me by Stevie Young of Summit Rescue, who along with Fraser MacDonald had helped me practice winching and lowering the RockPod at Ratho quarry. They had also loaned me some climbing kit, including one of the two IDs I'd lost in the storm. As I no longer had the IDs I had intended to use, this was a possible method of lowering the RockPod off Rockall. The hitch is essentially a normal alpine hitch with an added loop of rope across the face of the weighted line and back through the karabiner to increase the friction even further. Having practiced tying it a few times with paracord, I felt it may be good enough to use down the East cliff, as originally intended, rather than just the slope to the side, particularly as I would be able to put another karabiner, acting as a redirection point, into the system and would hopefully have some assistance on the rock to lower the pod off.

I continued in the afternoon recording geomagnetism readings along my previously described transects, in between fog banks. I'm not sure if I'm recording anything useful as I'm hardly getting any magnetic deviation when I lower the compass to the rock. It is very unfortunate that St. Andrew's were unable to lend me their magnetometer this year, as that would have been much more accurate, would have provided a defined figure, and would have removed any human error on my part. I've actually been able to create a very good grid for taking the readings, and feel that it's a shame that my effort and time on this task may not prove to be as useful as it might have been with the meter.

In any event, I have resolved to mark the most prominent baseline/transect intersections with some sort of bench mark, so that my measurements can be checked, repeated or corroborated in the future. Had I not already placed it, I might have used the brass survey marker that the Ordnance Survey gave me for this purpose, but as it is already resined into the summit, I'll mark it in some other way. In addition, while out finishing the survey, I realised that the grid I have created could be used to attempt to map out, as accurately as I can, the layout and features of Hall's Ledge, except for where it's covered by the RockPod. If I do run out of tasks before I leave, I may have an attempt at this too.

While I was out on the rock, a kittiwake landed at the opposite end of Hall's Ledge with a large brown stain across the back of its neck and onto its side, I saw it again later and noticed that both its wings are stained too. For the past few days I've also noticed another one with a similar stain covering its whole tail, which initially looked clumpy, but has now started to lighten and the feathers spread out again. I'm thinking that there must be a slick of oil or similar material on the water nearby which is affecting these birds, hopefully none fatally, and that this may also be the source of the rotting smell I mentioned previously and still catch in the air every now and again.

Once I'd finished the survey, as the weather had cleared and the wind dropped, I went up onto the summit for the first time in a few days, in order to look at the other aspect of the rock and see how many boats were about;

there was only one. I spent some time up there, photographing the summit, slopes, and Hall's Ledge from as many angles as I could and also attempting to take a series of photographs to link into panoramas of the slopes. It was calm and still and I had my thermal jacket on, so I was feeling comfortable up there and pondered for a while. Strangely I felt a sadness at the thought of leaving Rockall next week, which started to make me feel quite down. I thought about and believe that it's just because I think there is a lot more I could do and record here, some of which I had intended to do had I not lost my climbing hardware and had, for example, better scientific equipment like the magnetometer.

It's not often that anyone has this amount of time on Rockall, and I remember being surprised in the early days of planning the expedition, how little interest there was from the scientific community in me being able to carry out research here for them. St. Andrew's University came on board at the very last minute before last year's attempt to land, approaching me to record the geomagnetism, but I felt that even they didn't perhaps spend as long as they could have training me properly and giving the correct equipment, so that I could provide them with as much useful and accurate data as possible from my stay. I think this expedition has been, to some extent, an opportunity lost from that point of view, which is a shame. I only hope that I may have helped that future someone who may come here and build on my data, however inaccurate it is, using my surveys and benchmarks so that the data sets overlap.

Once I left the summit, I spent a while on the patio too, and there I got an overwhelming feeling of wanting to go home and move on with life. This project has taken up over five years of my life, and I really feel now that it's time to move on. Back inside the pod, I wrote up my daily diary. Being inside the pod for so much of the time over the past week and having been lying down on my back for much of that time, as hunching was hurting my back, I think I have started to develop the first stages of a pressure sore at the base of my spine, which is not only annoying but also means that I am having to compensate and lie in other awkward positions, moving regularly when a new piece of me starts to ache. I suppose this is what happens when you spend so much of your time confined in a cramped space, and hope that the weather is good enough that I can spend as much time as possible outside the pod in the run up to me leaving. This sore spot and the twitch below my eye, which has continued today, are not annoying but are testing my patience when there is not much else to dwell on.

Day 36 – 10th July

I've been waking up earlier in the mornings since the storm, and this morning was no different. However, the sea was probably the calmest it's been since I got here, in stark contrast to events just over a week ago. There was no wind at all, no waves, and a very slight swell. Today in fact was one of the days that Kilda Cruises initially proposed to come and get me off the rock after the storm; we would have had perfect conditions for it. As it is, they will be coming next week at some point, although they are awaiting the week's forecast on Sunday before making a decision.

I had a relatively relaxed morning, writing up my blog over a cup of tea (the dreaded concurrent activity creeping in), and didn't have breakfast until around 1000. Around 1025 I noticed a ship on the Southern horizon, and through the binoculars I could see that it was a large container ship with yellow cranes on its deck above a black hull. It was a long way off and moving East to West, so although it would be at its nearest when due South of me, it was not going to come close. I watched the gannets diving again, over a cup of coffee, and was able to see their bubble trail descend quite a long way under water before they surfaced. There were also a few minke back about, and I'm reasonably sure I counted four, although it might have been three!

Having written the first draft of my blog for the day, I went on to start writing a detailed description of Hall's Ledge. In the process of doing this, I realised that I needed to leave the pod to check a few things for the description, so thought that as the wind is due to build as the day progresses, I may as well start the measuring of the ledge at the same time. This took me the rest of the morning and part of the early afternoon to complete, and I'm confident that I have taken enough measurements to accurately draw the main features of the ledge, patio and ramp to scale when I get back. I then returned to the pod just before lunch and wrote up my notes afterwards, continuing with and finishing the description of Hall's Ledge in the process, by which time the wind had started to pick up from the south and the air became noticeably cooler. I spent the majority of the afternoon and evening reading, avoiding the cold wind as it built, and the damp air.

Day 37 – 11th July

I woke early again today, much to my annoyance, particularly as I'd stayed up later last night in an attempt to sleep late this morning. I'm not particularly tired, as a result of a lack of mental and physical exercise, but would as ever like to be cutting into my waking hours by sleeping more. The wind was still high when I got up, and it was noticeably cooler today, being only around twenty degrees inside the RockPod. Outside, with a stiff southerly breeze, which turned to the west as the morning progressed, the wind chill made it feel much cooler and I sat with my woolly hat and Buff around my neck for much of the morning, while I read and drank hot drinks.

I started my fourth water carrier this morning, but decided not to put the empty one out with the others as it would not make a significant impact on my space, being now lined up in a row with other full ones along the end of the pod. Today is also clean underwear day again; when I go to get these from the barrels later I'm going to check whether I have any more resin left, which I don't think I have, so that I can reinforce the remaining plaques on

Rockall before I leave. The weather is supposed to improve slightly after lunch, with the wind speed dropping and moving around to the west, so I'm planning to go out to do my daily tasks then.

Having read until mid-morning, I felt inspired to do my daily tasks and so headed out of the pod before lunch, not after as planned. I first found and put into the pod my remaining clean underwear and socks along with a clean pair of trousers, which would be my first clean pair since I got here! I then got out the drill, changed the battery, and put the dead battery and charger away in a barrel as I can't think that I'll be needing them again. The first job with the drill was to mark the cross and the numeral VI at that transect intersection with the drill's chisel bit and action. This went well and was quite easy and not too obvious unless you were looking for it, so I went on to also mark the intersections at transect three (III) and nine (IX). This will enable someone in the future to lay the whole baseline as I had it and find the remaining transects from these points as they are all one metre apart.

I then put the drill away and looked for any remaining resin, which as I suspected I didn't find as it was with all the 'spares' in number three barrel which was washed away. I still had the remnants of the original cartridge that I used to bolt the turbine mount and plaques in, and there was some in that. Changing the nozzle, I was surprised and pleased that there was enough to seal around the whole of the plaque on the summit, particularly as I had previously scraped and cleaned around it for this purpose, which had left it in a weakened positioned had it not been sealed, and I also filled the vacant bolt hole in the plaque, leaving an overlapping plug of resin in the hope that this will help hold it down, or at least stop water getting under it. There still being some resin left, I filled and tidied some small gaps around the plaques I put up a few weeks ago, and also filled the gap around the bent Collinox fixing on the patio, which had appeared after the storm. There is still a little bit of resin left, which I'll save in case something else crops up that needs it before I leave.

Finally, before returning to the pod, I practiced the super munter hitch in the location at the edge of the cliff that I would be using it if I am to lower the pod down the main cliff. I tied it easily and the setup, with a return in the rope to create even more friction and control, was easy to rig. However, even unloaded, I could not pull the rope through the hitch with all my strength. This makes me think that a normal munter with return may be sufficient, and I re-tied the system with the normal hitch and was impressed how much friction was in it. I'll think further on this, and will also try both systems again before I need them, in order to help me make a final decision. Certainly, if there is another person on the ledge with me to help lower the pod, at the moment, I think that the normal munter will be fine.

Although the wind did drop as forecast in the afternoon, the air was wet, with a hazy drizzle. This combined with the cool air meant that I was confined to the pod for the afternoon, reading and doing some Italian lessons, so was glad I'd done my jobs this morning. A large number of gannets were around again this morning, and as the afternoon progressed they started to land on the patio and ramp. I shooed them away when they did, as I dislike their cackling and don't want them getting too used to being near me because, as mentioned previously, they are pretty fearsome close up. They seemed happy enough to land back down on the water, fighting amongst themselves and bobbing around in the swell. Once the drizzle stopped, I wrapped up warm and sat up in the pod with the top hatch open, watching as the gannets dived for fish, amazed at the height that they dive from and how they sometimes invert during the dive in an effort to track the fish they've seen shimmering beneath the water.

This afternoon I got very bored for the first time. I read for a while, but was bored of that too. I don't know whether it's the prospect of going home next week, but I really now want to leave, and I'm craving actual human contact and conversation, the easy ability to walk outside or turn on a tap. I'm hoping this is a passing phase as I don't want to be like this until I leave; that would make the last few days feel like forever. I'm thinking it's probably manifesting because of the prospect of going home, the cold miserable day, and the closeness of being able to see my family. It may also be, of course, because I have been waking up earlier the past few days, giving more hours in the day to fill, so that my normal tasks and routines are being completed with at least an hour and a half to spare. This being the case, if I continue to wake up early, the next couple of days are going to be hard as they are forecast to be yet more windy, meaning that I will be inclined to go out even less still.

I'm not sure how Tom McClean managed it with none of the modern technologies that I have. I don't know if he had children when he was here, but one of the hardest things has been hearing second hand about the new experiences my son has been having while I've been on Rockall and the things he has been doing. Tom only had a VHF radio, and can't have used that much as trawler men are busy people. He wouldn't have seen or spoken to his family for the whole time he was here; but perhaps he was used to that, having been in the army and the SAS, being away from family for prolonged periods of time – I am not. Similarly, I live in a different age, where I'm used to being able to call people up easily, remember that there weren't even mobile phones in Tom's day. Similarly iPods and e-books didn't exist, although I think there were probably more English language radio stations broadcasting on shortwave then than now.

Day 38 - 12th July

Thankfully, finally, I went to sleep fairly quickly last night and didn't wake up until just before 0900, rising shortly after that time. The weather was dull, misty, and wet, but fortunately the wind was from the North, so I was sheltered. There seems to be a few more terns about today, and their high pitched chirp reminds me of birds back home in my garden.

I strung breakfast out past 1000, and then played cards and read for a while. The weather cleared around 1230, so much so that that I was too warm and had to remove my pullover for the first time in a few days. Off to the east I could see breakers in the same location as I've seen them previously, and so I am now fairly convinced that this must be the location of Helen's Reef[27]. However, this spell was short lived as the mist rolled back in quickly. The oil stained kittiwake has been sitting on the Eastern step for a few hours, looking sorry for itself. It can fly, but I assume it's either tired from having clogged feathers or weak from not being able to fish effectively. Hopefully it'll clean up in the coming days. His plight made me think sadly about the young starling that joined me just before the storm. I've tried not to think about it as emotions are extreme out here, but I suspect that he won't have made it through the storm unless by some miracle he was blown all the way to Faroe!

There were a number of clear spells during the early afternoon, interspersed with wet banks of fog and mist rolling through. The wind speed appeared to pick up from the north, as evidenced by the turbine turning faster, and I was glad to be sheltered from it. Each time I popped my head out of the RockPod I managed to time it with when the only trawler out here at the moment, K121 'Keila', was passing to the south. She must be on quite a short loop as in the past boats have taken much longer to go back and forth than she appeared to be doing. Seeing her made me wonder whether PD340 'Ocean Venture', who were following me on Twitter and whom I spoke to on the VHF, would be back out here before I leave, or whether she's on other fishing grounds now.

---

[27] I confirmed from charts on my return that this was indeed Helen's Reef.

The sun came out for a while after lunch, so I took the opportunity to go out for a 'walk' around the rock. I did some exercises on the patio, and then went up onto the summit to check the resin I'd placed yesterday, and take yet more photographs from differing angles. I then went down to the eastern step and sat there for a while, out of the breeze, enjoying the warmer weather before pondering the pod-lowering conundrum some more. I'm now veering towards lowering it down the cliff face on a normal munter hitch with return. After that, for a change in scenery, I moved over to the seat at the west step. When I got there, I noticed that the oiled kittiwake was stood in the middle of the patio, and it didn't move as I sat down. I chatted to it for a while; it looked fairly subdued, not even moving, although raising its head when I stood to look round the corner of the plaque wall. It later flew off, came back for a while, then moved to the east step as the wind moved round, so it's obviously still fairly active. In the latter half of the afternoon the sun came out, and I sat on the deck of the RockPod with my legs across the top hatch opening, watching the gannets diving for almost an hour.

I hadn't read much today, so I finally finished Malcolm X's autobiography, and will now have to decide what to read next! The mob of gannets that were fishing earlier decided they wanted a rest and kept landing on the patio; I shooed them off again as they were cackling too much! By early evening the cloud had come back over and the wind moved round to the west so I was no longer in the lee of the rock. As a result the temperature dropped, which is a shame as it looks like it might be a fair evening, but will be too cold to be out in. I did, however, spot a second trawler, although it is a long way off to the west, so I can't make out if it's one I've seen before or not, and in the early evening a second container ship appeared, plying the same route as the one I saw a few days ago, along the southern horizon. Before bed, I found another two ticks, one on the floor of the pod and one on my leg. Neither lasted long once spotted, but thankfully both appeared not to have consumed anything for quite a while.

Day 39 – 13th July

As forecast, the wind picked up during the night and I slept fitfully, although gladly I managed until just before 0900 again. The wind was not much higher than yesterday, but was now from the south west, so that I was no longer sheltered on Hall's Ledge. The waves had also increased in height overnight, and were from the same direction as the wind, which meant that the odd spray reached higher up the rock. I had, however, slept through the forecast peak of both wind and waves between 0400 and 0700, and both were now supposed to slowly decrease through to tomorrow and then stay relatively low for the remainder of my stay. As a result of the wind and waves, I suspect, the gannets were back on the ramp when I awoke; one of which has green string wrapped around its neck, although it doesn't appear to be the worse for wear for it. I spoke firmly to them, pointing out that they would have the whole rock to themselves soon enough, and they thankfully moved on.

Having finished a book yesterday, and not finding any more autobiographies that took my fancy on my laptop, I started reading Bill Bryson's 'Neither Here, Nor There: Travels in Europe'. I have read 'Notes from a Small Island' previously and remembered it being funny and an easy read. The wind continued for much of the morning, although it did brighten up. When I popped my head out of the hatch mid-morning, I was pleased to see that the oiled kittiwake, which I have now imaginatively named 'Kitti', was still with me, and another boat I'd seen before, K373 'Aalskere', has appeared to the east. The wind cannot be much higher than yesterday, but it makes a significant difference, even at the mid to high 20mph range, when you are not sheltered from it at all.

Around midday, having read and giggled as hoped, for much of the morning, I made a cup of hot coffee and the gas canister ran out again just as it boiled. Changing the canister, I mused whether this would be the first of many things I would be doing for last time here before I leave?

It rained more than was forecast during the early afternoon, but each of the banks of showers passed through quickly, and I usually saw them coming so could close the top hatch as necessary. After reading for most of the day, and being consequently static, I was pleased that in the mid-afternoon there was a longer dry spell, so I took the opportunity to stand and do some resistance exercises with the Thera-band, while watching the next load of rain-depositing clouds roll in from the south-west, and being watched by a seal.

I knew that the main battery was fairly full as the charge controller had been dumping heat when I woke up this morning. As it was windy all day, and I knew that in a few days I would be disconnecting the turbine, I took the opportunity to charge and discharge a few pieces of equipment in an effort to get the batteries, some of which were fairly new, holding their charge as well as possible. This included my neighbour Ben's GoPro camera he had leant me, the VHF radio, and the laptop. I also charged up the batteries for the Leica GNSS receiver, as I thought it likely that I would be running the second data collection tomorrow.

Checking my emails at the end of the day I got a bit of a shock when a lady emailed me asking if her husband could join the boat coming out to get me on the 23rd, which is over a week away! I quickly phoned Angus of Kilda Cruises as I hadn't been told when he was coming, but had expected it to be this week around the 17th. He had fortunately given her the wrong date, and confirmed that he is currently planning to leave Harris on Thursday night (17th) arriving here on Friday; I estimate he'll arrive around midday, as they will not be leaving until after 2200 due to the availability of the skipper. Confirming that they would indeed be coming for me this week was a relief, but although I had tried not to, I had got Thursday in the back of my mind for leaving, which means an extra day here to deal with mentally.

Day 40 – 14th July

So today I've equalled Tom McClean's twenty nine year solo record!

I've written previously about how his experience would have been very different to mine, and I expect his boredom threshold must have been much higher than mine too. I can't, however, believe that he had to weather a storm like the one I had two weeks ago, as I can't see how his plywood box, tied down as it was with ropes and pitons, would have survived it. That being said, I have great respect for the man. I don't feel euphoric, perhaps that will come tomorrow when I set a new record, but today I do feel very much that I could do longer if the three factors of weather, food, and boat availability had allowed. I'm not too disappointed that I will not complete my planned sixty days, but part of me would have liked to have beaten both records by more than just a couple of days.

Reproduced with permission Simon Wright

I had another reasonable lie in this morning until just before 0900, and the weather was as forecast: wind from the North West, so that I was sheltered on the ledge, low waves, and fairly clear skies. After breakfast, and having charged up the batteries yesterday, I decided that I would start the second GNSS survey. So, I had to get all the equipment out of its barrel and set it up on the summit, using the same survey anchor, which I'd left in situ. I also packed away the battery charger for the unit as I won't be needing it again, which is the start, I suppose, of packing up. This didn't take long; in fact it should have taken about five minutes, but I managed to stretch it out to around fifteen. In the process of doing this, I noted that there were some dregs of water in the bottom of the one remaining large barrel, which I will use to get the main battery off the rock when I leave, so I drained this and left it upside down to air, while I set up the receiver and did some other jobs.

The GNSS receiver will stay in place again for twenty four hours, or until the batteries run out, whichever is the sooner. Leica hope that by cross referencing both sets of readings, taken a month apart when the relevant satellites are in different positions, they will be able to calculate a more accurate position and height for the rock than they would be able to from just one set of readings[28].

Having set up the receiver, I returned to the RockPod and collected my note book, compass and pens so that I could collect a few more orientated rock samples for St. Andrew's University. I had lengthened my life line by adding a climbing sling with a karabiner to the end, which allowed me to go further down the North face than I can normally, but unfortunately not as far as if I'd still had all my climbing hardware. I collected another three samples, making a total of ten, which I hope is enough for their purposes; they are from a variety of locations and aspects of the rock, and so I hope they will prove to be of some interest. Again, I think with more training I could perhaps have increased the usefulness of the samples, but they will all add something to the story of Rockall nonetheless. I then decided to make an attempt at drawing the back wall above Hall's Ledge with its characteristic cracks and the rough position of the anchors and core sample holes marked on it. I was pleased how this turned out, and may be able to use it to record the angle of the main cracks for St. Andrew's too, as they have asked me to do this if I

---

[28] Appendix B

can. I had an early lunch as I had a diarised interview with Inmarsat at 1400, which went smoothly.

Shortly afterwards the James Clark Ross came over the VHF from about two miles to the North West. I had a good chat with them and asked them to record some video footage from the ship. Again they came very close on the south of the rock, doing a full 360 degree turn almost on the spot, while they waved and photographed me. They were here for over half an hour, before moving east to their same survey spot as before, and then off back to Scotland. Unfortunately, during their visit, I dropped my camera and broke it. This is not the end of the world, as my video camera will also take photographs and at a higher resolution, but it just goes to show that you should always have a backup.

I read for the remainder of the afternoon, finishing the current Bill Bryson book, and commencing 'Notes from a Small Island', which I've read before but some years ago. Unfortunately, in the early evening I felt a bit ill, with an aching stomach and lots of wind. I'm hoping its nothing serious brewing, and it seemed to pass after a lot of farting! The wind turned to the west during the afternoon as well, which meant it is onto the pod again, and is forecast to stay on the pod, from the West or South, for the remainder of my stay, which is not ideal, but it should be at relatively low speeds, so not too inconvenient, I hope.

Day 41 – 15th July

Today marks a new solo record for the occupation of Rockall. No-one has ever been here on their own for as long as I have today! That's a pretty good feeling, although it's obviously really just another day here, with the usual routines. I have, however, got a tiny bottle of champagne which I think I'll have with my supper to celebrate!

When I eventually got to sleep last night, I slept well and awoke to blue skies and a southerly breeze, as forecast. I think I've said it before, but the Windguru online forecast has been very accurate; it has three hour bandings and it's usually spot on with changes in wind speed, direction, etc. After breakfast, the first job was to take down and pack away the GNSS receiver which I'd put up and started yesterday morning. The battery had already run out by 1030, but having checked and backed up the memory card, there is a good amount of data on there for comparison with the first readings I got a month ago. I packed the receiver and its pole away in a barrel, as I will not be needing it again, and checked yet again how much space is in the other barrels for when I pack up properly in a couple of days' time. It looks like I'll have enough space for everything, including the charge controller, which came on to Rockall bolted inside the RockPod, but which I want to take off in a barrel in case I have to drop the pod; I think the shock of the impact with the water would break the controller.

As its forecast to be a dry and breezy day, I decided that this might be my last chance to take a mould of Tom McClean's carving in the rock, especially as most of tomorrow will be taken up with dismantling the wind turbine, and I'll be packing everything else the next day. I did a bit of researching on moulding rocks before I came out, and decided that the best option was to use liquid latex, reinforced with muslin. I was very pleased how the first few coats of the latex went on and dried; I left about an hour between each coat. While they were drying, I did a few exercises on the patio and had a general wander about the rock, taking yet more photographs on the video camera from angles I couldn't remember if I'd taken from before, and adding a bit more detail to my sketch of the back wall that I drew yesterday.

I proceeded to add another coat to the mould every hour as the wind was drying each layer out nicely. This had the unfortunate effect of making me watch the clock, which always means that the time goes slower. I noticed in the afternoon that, in addition to the gannets now insisting on landing on the lower levels of the rock and squawking with their ugly screech, the guillemots seem to have started to move back in on the summit plateau. I greeted them kindly, and informed them that I would be taking the turbine down tomorrow, and that they would then have the summit to themselves once again.

Last thing last night, and again today, I saw yet another new bird. I have not been able to get a good photograph of it yet, but it has a black beak and orange legs, a black and white head with brown skull cap, white lower body, and its wings and back are speckled brown and black. Also, its call is a high pitched shrill. Hopefully I'll get a good photo and then perhaps someone online will be able identify it for me[29]. I spent the afternoon reading for a while, exercising with the Thera-band before putting it away for the final time, and applying coats of latex to the mould. Later on, I went over the summit to the north side of the rock as it was in the lee and I could sit there

---

[29] I identified it on my return home as a Ringed Plover.

and watch the trawlers plying back and forth without the incessant wind, which was nice. I even got a bit too warm and had to remove my jacket while I sat there!

I finished the day by peeling back the mould, which I was pleased to see had taken the shape of Tom's carving well and came off the rock very easily. Latex moulds are apparently pretty tough, but I am going to seal it in a bag before packing it away to transport home. After supper I treated myself to the tiny bottle of champagne to celebrate my solo record, which had chilled fairly well in the cool breeze.

I was also very lucky in that the 'Aalskere' came very close past the rock crossing from one side of Rockall to the other. I had a good chat with their skipper over the VHF, and learnt that the area that most of the boats have been running back and forth in to the east of the rock is known as The Trench, and that all the boats here are fishing for squid. He said that for the rest of the year there is no-one out here, but for four or five weeks in June and July they come here for the squid, for which there is no quota, which helps them a lot. The Aalskere has been away from its home port in Orkney for five and a half weeks, fishing here the whole time apart from a couple of trips to Ullapool to land their catch, which is where they were when my storm hit.

Day 42 – 16th July

I awoke to a still day, which was good news as I'd planned to take the wind turbine down today, and although I could stop it in high winds, it would make working up on the exposed summit more comfortable. There were many more birds out in front of the ledge fishing than I've seen to date, with so many gannets diving it was a wonder that they didn't hit each other. I had seen lots of shearwaters and a pair of the mystery brown and white speckled birds that I saw one of yesterday. Today I equalled Greenpeace's group occupation record set in 1997, seventeen years ago. It's odd to think that tomorrow I will have been here longer than anyone in history, but after five years of planning and preparation, astonishing too.

Yet again, I was feeling this morning that I could do longer here, but the other rational side of me remembers the storm. I'm not confident that the RockPod hasn't taken some unseen damage, and certainly mentally, I don't think I could go through that experience again. It's also not just about me, the pod and the food supply; there's no guarantee that at sixty days the boat could come and get me immediately due to the weather at the time. The last thing I want is to be stuck here with no food. Better to take my chances, break the records and get home safely. It may be that the fact I haven't pushed the records out further as I originally planned leaves the door open for someone else to come and break my solo record. In fact Iain Maciver told me last night that someone in Ireland is already talking about doing exactly that; but that is the thing about records: they're there to be broken, which is exactly what I've done with this trip. Tom McClean himself said that he didn't think his solo record would ever be broken and I proved him wrong yesterday. Good luck to anyone who wants to have a go; it's not easy, involves complicated logistics, and just organising an expedition like this takes up your life even before you land, assuming the weather allows it.

I spent the morning taking down the wind turbine as planned. It was far easier and took a lot less time than I had thought it might, partly due to the favourable weather, but also I think because having done it a few times now and having thought through the process in my head for a few days before, I had a good system in place. I started by stopping the turbine and tying off the blades so that it wasn't generating any power, which I could check by looking at the charge light on the controller in the RockPod. I then disconnected the waterproof junction box linking the turbine output wire to the controller input wire and put that away in a barrel. Next I had to take each of the six blades off the turbine head, which I did carefully so as not to drop the bolts, placing them in a bag within my one remaining large barrel and putting the blades in the barrel too, so that I could lower them safely from the summit down to Hall's Ledge. Having removed the blades, I also took off the tail, placing that with the blades and getting all those pieces of the turbine down first. I threaded the power cable back through the Collinox anchors, which I had used to stop the cable flapping in the wind, removing the cable ties that had held it in place as I went.

Back on the summit, I loosened and then disconnected each of the guy wires in turn, so that I could lean the mast over and pull out the turbine head and attached cable. That went fairly to plan, except for the fact that one side of the base plate that I had resin bolted into the rock came loose and so I had to dash as fast as I could from behind the light housing to catch the mast and turbine head as they fell towards the ledge! That saved, I leant the whole apparatus down so that it was lying along the summit and easily pulled out the head and the cable through the mast pole. I tied up the cable with cable ties, and put the head with its cable into a large dry bag which I slung over my shoulders to take down to the ledge. The turbine head had come onto Rockall protected in a large barrel, but as I now only had one, which was for the battery; the head will have to go down in the dry bag, which I think will be strong enough for that one trip.

Once the turbine head was down, I went back up to the summit to unbolt the mast and wrap up the guy wires, which I duct-taped to the mast once it was back down at the pod. With the summit clear, all that remained was the cable into the pod and the charge controller. I needed to unscrew the grommet that sealed the hole where the cable penetrated the pod and pulled the cable through to the inside. I then sealed the grommet with silicone so that water did not get into the pod as it travelled to the boat or on the deck on the way back to land. The charge controller easily unbolted from its mount inside the RockPod, and I again coiled up the cables, having disconnected the battery, secured them with cable ties and placed the controller and cables into the last large barrel for safe transport. Having competed today's big task, I had a mug of coffee to celebrate a job well done.

Once that was finished, I waited for a reporter to call me on the satellite phone as arranged yesterday, but they didn't call, so I went round my Raumer hanging plates and positioned them at the best angles for safety that I could get them and gave the bolts a good thwack with the hammer to make sure they're properly secure, just in case anyone decides to rely on them in the future. It was a shock how much space there now appeared to be up on the summit plateau, with the turbine having been removed, and not having to dodge the spinning blades or hop over the guy wires. I spent a while up there just enjoying being able to walk about a bit, albeit not very far, on a flat surface for the first time in weeks.

This afternoon I downloaded the data from my weather station base unit to the laptop, which proved interesting: the last time it recorded was in the half hour window between 2200 and 2230 on the 1st July, when it recorded a wind speed of 47.2 miles per hour, with a gust of 54.8 miles per hour from the South. The forecast was for it to get worse after that, peaking at around 0100 the next morning at a speed of just 40 miles per hour! Assuming that the peak was at the forecast time, I extrapolated from the trend that in fact the wind speed was around 55 miles per hour at its peak, with a maximum gust of almost 60 miles per hour. I can't confirm this, but that would make it a Force 10 Storm! I also noticed that the hinge on the main hatch has a crack in it, which is not great, but it only had to last a couple more days, so it should be alright.

At the end of the day, I checked my emails as usual, only to find out that Kilda Cruises have moved their departure to come and collect me back by twenty four hours, from the day after tomorrow, Thursday, to Friday. When I saw the forecast last night, I half suspected they might do this, as the winds are behind them if they leave on Friday evening, as now planned, drop to almost nothing at the time they would arrive here, and then turn back to the west, so that it will be behind the boat all the way home too. This will make for quicker journeys both ways, will hopefully therefore save me something on fuel costs, and also means an extra day on my occupation record, but does have the down side that I have another day here which I have to mentally absorb and also, having taken down the wind turbine today, means that I may be short on power come Friday night.

Having said that, I was blessed again tonight with another glorious evening, and so sat out on the patio for a while after supper, drinking my hot chocolate before going to bed.

Day 43 – 17th July

I didn't sleep well, not helped by some inaudible chatter over the VHF around 0430, and then being woken again at 0630 by a radio call for me from the Woods Hole Oceanographic Institution vessel 'Knorr' who were just off Rockall to the South East and had stopped to say hello. This was very nice of them, and I don't want to sound ungrateful as it's great to see and speak to people out here, but right then I could have done with another two hours sleep! I suspect the earlier chatter was them too. Anyway, we had a good talk over the VHF and I was invited to tea at their base in Oban, before amazingly they set off lots of fireworks on their rear deck, which I took to be in honour of today being the longest anyone has ever been on Rockall.

I did manage to get around another hour's sleep after they headed off to Iceland having, they told me, been laying moorings around Rockall; which is interesting that anyone would need a mooring out here. I supposed it may be to fix points for future surveys. The morning weather was glorious again, with clear blue skies, and yet another first for me here, the moon was still out and visible.

This morning, after a very drawn out breakfast due to the early wakeup call, I didn't want to fully pack up as I would have nothing to do tomorrow with departure having been delayed by a day, so I put a few more bits and bobs away that it was clear I wouldn't need in the next twenty four hours, and found places in the barrels for the turbine blades, which had been in the battery barrel temporarily, but needed to be moved as the weight of the battery might break them in transit.

I amused myself for part of the afternoon by looking back at some of the photos and video I have taken while here and as I stumbled across it on the laptop, I read aloud The Island of Rockall Act (1972), much to the chagrin of the birds that were round about. I sat on the lee side of the rock for a while again, and then nursing a suddenly aching stomach, I spent most of the rest of the day reading in the RockPod, finishing my current Bryson book, and moving on to 'I'm a Stranger Here Myself', by the same author. Every now and again, I caught myself looking up out of the hatch for the wind turbine, which was no longer there, to get an indication of wind speed and direction. It's odd not being able to use that facility, and instead having to put my head out of the hatch. The wind has been from the East today, and is forecast to remain so for the rest of my stay, which is unusual in my experience here as this is the only direction it really hasn't been from. This has resulted in a couple of accidents while peeing without paying attention!

Surprisingly, to me at least, having been here longer than anyone in history has not been the celebratory event that I had expected. I suppose that having planned and prepared for this day for so long, I had built it up subconsciously into some sort of tangible event, whereas in reality it is just another day. I'm still on my own which makes it difficult to celebrate substantially, and most people will be going about their normal daily routines completely oblivious to what I have achieved today. I am really pleased that I have broken both the records, particularly having been so severely tested by the weather, but in truth I'm looking forward to going home and my main focus is now preparing for my departure, packing up, and getting back to shore safely.

There's not really very much for me to do here now anyway, and I thought about how I would have amused myself had I been staying for another two weeks as originally planned; yet more reading and pondering was my first thought, Italian and harmonica lessons my second. There was always fishing; I have brought a rod, lures and reel, but have not got them out as I did not have a reliably clean place to prepare any fish I caught; I didn't want to get ill and didn't want to try and unhook and return a fish safely from this height that I wasn't going to eat. If really bored, I would probably have had a go though, if nothing else but to pass the time. Also, had I not lost my climbing hardware in the storm, I had intended to explore further down and around the sides of Rockall, but was now unable to do that. Had I been able to, I may have collected more rock samples and geomagnetism readings in the process.

Day 44 – 18th July

It took me quite a while to get to sleep last night; surprisingly, as I was very tired from the night before and an early wake up call. I did, however, manage to sleep until around 0830, and woke to be greeted by a calm but misty day. I was hoping for a better day, like yesterday morning with light winds and sunshine for my last full day, but it was not meant to be. During breakfast, the Aalskere came quite close to the South of me, but didn't call on the VHF; I think they were having an experimental trawl for squid as they had their nets out and I haven't seen them do that in that location before.

The big job for the day was packing away most of my remaining kit into the barrels and sorting out the various straps which I've been using to strap the barrels down, but which will soon be needed for lowering the pod off Rockall, and then lifting it onto the boat, Orca 3. I had hoped that this would all take at least most of the morning, but as ever, despite going slowly, I was finished in about half an hour! Having changed into the last of my clean clothes and underwear for going home, which I have been saving so as not to stink out the boat or scare my family when I get back, I packed away non-essentials such as dirty clothes, what few remaining rations I have, some electronics and tools, and my medical kit. None are too difficult to get back out if I need them in the next twenty four hours, due to the amount of space I now have as a result of consuming rations, loo roll, and losing kit.

There is still some stuff left in the RockPod, which I will probably need in the next day: the main battery, electronics for last minute charging, laptop, VHF, binoculars, Isatphone and BGAN for example, along with my stove, some food, and all my remaining water which I will pour out at the last minute when the boat arrives. I have decided that I will transport the water carriers off Rockall and back to shore inside the RockPod; when full they were lifted onto the rock individually and travelled here on the deck. They will be very light once empty and it will save the extra hassle and time of lowering them down and loading them onto the boat. Similarly, I may also put all the ratchet straps straight into the pod when I disconnect them, as although they are heavier, I don't think it will make a significant difference to the pod weight, and there is probably not enough space left in barrels for all of them too.

Around mid-morning, although the drizzle had stopped, it was still very calm and the fog closed in so that I could hear the boats nearby but could only see twenty to thirty metres all around. If it's like this tomorrow it will pose a bit of a challenge for the boat and ferrying my kit from the rock back to it, but they'll have a couple of RIBs on board, so they should be able to stand off the rock in the boat with no problems. Around 1100 the skipper of the Aalskere came on the VHF and we had a really long chat for almost an hour about fishing, fish stocks, quotas, etc. It was really interesting to get some background to what's going on out here and generally with fishing in and around Scotland. He, as I've read in the press, thinks that the current scientific data is about three years out of date as regards fish number recovery, and he gave the example of cod in the North Sea, where in 2007 it took them all year to catch around forty five tonnes of cod, but last year they caught more than that in a single three hour trawl!

It was good to learn that there is almost zero discard from squid fishing, perhaps some sand eels, but that's about it. Also, because they have increased the size of the mesh in their nets, there's very little undersized fish caught now either. He admits that a few years ago the fishing fleet was definitely catching too much fish, as stocks were dropping rapidly, but he believes that they are now at or rapidly approaching a very sustainable level of fishing due to the advances in fishing gear, but also, somewhat sadly, because of the lack of fishing boats around today.

After a light lunch the fog thankfully slowly cleared and the wind dropped as it moved further round to the east, so that I could stand and take in the view in relative calm. I decided on another cup of tea, partly because it takes time to make, but also because I seem to have turned drinking tea into a very good way to pass the time. The sea got steadily calmer as the day progressed and the view stretched further, finally reaching the horizon. Watching the birds, seals and whales in this environment brought an involuntary smile to my face, and I was finally again glad to be here and to have had this experience; although I am very much looking forward to going home. I spent some time on the now empty summit, taking in the 360 degree view, the three trawlers in the distance, and thinking about all I have done, measured and photographed since I arrived. I've left my mark in the form of the survey markers and plaques I'll leave behind, but hope that I have also recorded a little more about this place, to add to James Fisher's and others' records.

I read in the late afternoon as it got cooler and the rain started, before charging up some vital bits of kit for the journey home tomorrow, like the satellite phone and GoPro camera. In the evening, having sent my last Tweet from the rock, the weather cleared a bit and I could stand and take in the scene. My first Arctic Tern appeared, which was lovely, but unfortunately a Volvic bottle wrapper floated past at around the same time. Quite a juxtaposition, but also peculiarly very Rockall, it being a "Realm of the sea"[30] and yet still affected by man's presence, even all the way out here.

---

[30] Ben Fogle

Day 45 – 19ˢᵗ July

I didn't sleep at all well, dropping off after 0200 and waking again around 0645. I had a lot of tasks on my mind, and was genuinely excited at the prospect of getting off the rock. I eventually got up about 0730, had a light breakfast and a cup of tea, while awaiting a call on the Istaphone2 from Kilda Cruises with their estimated time of arrival. Angus Campbell telephoned at 0805, saying that they were three and a half hours away and enquiring about the sea state and whether there was any fog at Rockall, as they were in a bank of it. Having waited until I knew that they were within striking distance of the rock, I packed the remaining bits of kit like my stove, sleeping bag and satellite phone into the barrels and moved them from their position behind the RockPod to the Eastern Step at the end of Hall's Ledge, above the East Cliff, where they would be lowered from, and prepared the ropes that I would be using to get the barrels down.

I then removed some of the restraining ratchet straps from the South side of the pod, and poured away two containers full of drinking water; not all of it at this stage as something could still go wrong and I didn't want to be left with no drinking water at all. As I would be hand lowering the pod down the cliff and it would then have to be craned onto Orca 3, I wanted to evenly distribute the weight inside the pod, and I also restrain some of the kit inside it so that the weight was fairly evenly balanced for the crane. The water containers and ratchet straps, which would be travelling back to shore inside the RockPod as I had fewer barrels, would then not all slide to one end as it was lowered down the cliff.

The weather was breezy, dry, and fairly calm, which would provide good conditions for the Orca's crew to land on the rock and for getting my equipment off. Although there had been high winds in the night, the forecast was for these to tail off in the morning, to around twelve miles per hour, with gusts of sixteen, from the South East, waves of 1.7 metres, and swell of 1.2 metres.

While completing my final tasks before departure, I was pleased to see both the minke whales and a seal, which I felt had come to see me off; certainly the birds seemed keen to claim the rock back! In the end, I had a lot more equipment inside the pod when it was lowered than when it went onto Rockall, including all my water containers and the ratchet straps, but I had reasoned that the weight would be less of an issue for lowering it than lifting, and by being inside the RockPod it would mean that there were less individual items to lower down and then get onto the boat, which should speed the process up and make it easier and safer for everyone involved.

Orca 3 radioed via the VHF from around nine miles out to test communications, but this also meant that I could remove further straps from the pod and pour away more water. At five miles, they couldn't hear me very well, so they called again at around three miles, at which point I could see their wake with the naked eye, but not the boat itself. They arrived about 1130, and having removed the final ratchet straps, I went up onto the summit to wave and greet them.

The plan was for the boat to drop an anchor, which took a while as the bottom around Rockall varies from sandy to smooth hard rock, and then put two RIBs into the water. They wanted to take the opportunity to land a couple of people, including a TV camera man, which would also help me as I thought I would need extra hands for lowering the RockPod. Chris Murray, the winch man author of the first book I'd read on Rockall, and the camera man got on safely and made their way up to Hall's Ledge, and we then hauled up the camera kit. I started to lower down the barrels of my kit while they set up for the first ever TV interview on Rockall.

When it came to lowering the RockPod down Rockall, I had finally decided on a simple munter hitch with a single change of direction in the rope in front of the hitch, which would add friction to the system, but also allow me to be away from the edge of the cliff and behind the pod as it was lowered. While two men held the rope taught, feeding out slack, I pushed the pod to the edge of the cliff and onto its balance point. Joining the other two on the rope, we went to lower the pod and immediately realised that there was enough friction in the system for me to lower the pod on my own, and almost one handed, which was great as it left them free to film me lowering it. This was a relief as I had thought that I might have to drop the pod down the cliff, and hope for the best. One of the tenders collected the RockPod at the bottom of the cliff and towed it over to the boat, and after raising an 'Isle of Harris' flag (Rockall is in the District of Harris[31]), we descended one by one, with me going last, down climbing the North side of the rock until at sea level and then jumping into the water to be rapidly collected by the RIB.

I was quickly on board Orca 3, where I was greeted by both Angus Campbell and Smith, 'The Angii', congratulated by the crew, and handed a bottle of fizz with which to celebrate. We remained at Rockall for about an hour, while the RockPod and tenders were craned aboard, photographs were taken, and I completed a further interview for television, before setting off for St. Kilda where we expected to arrive around 0100, and rest until first light.

---

[31] Island of Rockall Act 1972

As we prepared to leave I was struck with a sense of disappointment. Part of me didn't want to leave that spot, and I knew that I hadn't achieved all I had hoped to in terms of recording the features of the rock or pushing out the records as far as I'd planned. In a way, Rockall had beaten me, forcing me to leave early, and yet as I departed, and it shrunk to a speck on the horizon, I knew that I had left a part of myself therewith the wind, the seabirds, and the whalesthat I hoped to return for one day.

The crossing back was uneventful, and I woke in Village Bay to the smell of curry coming from the galley. After a late supper, I went back to sleep until dawn, when we cruised through the stacks around the archipelago before heading in to Leverburgh on the Isle of Harris. We motored into the harbour around 0950, and it was brilliant to see my little boy jumping up and down with excitement at the first sight of "Daddy's boat", and then at seeing me. Getting that huge hug from him and my wife felt amazing and I felt finally that I was safely back to shore.

There were a few interviews to be done on the quay, though thankfully not as many as I had feared as I was tired from the journey back and lack of sleep, and really just wanted to get somewhere quiet with my family.

Unfortunately the van that had been organised to take the RockPod and barrels to their temporary storage had not been left as I had come off the rock early, so there followed a series of phone calls, and the pod was moved for twenty four hours to the bunkhouse in Leverburgh, with the barrels going by a different vehicle north to Luskentyre. Once they were secure, we continued up to Tarbert, went to a hotel and I had a very lengthy shower, the first proper wash I'd had for forty five days, followed by a freshly cooked meal.

POSTSCRIPT

We eventually flew south from Stornoway two days after landing in Harris. My original plan was for a friend, Jamie, to bring up a van to take all my gear and the RockPod back home at the end of the expedition. As I had to come off Rockall early, neither he nor the van were available, and so everything was put into temporary storage at a friend's parents' croft at Luskentyre on Harris. Once home, I started the process of updating my website, contacting sponsors, returning loaned equipment and completing interviews with newspapers and television. A week later, and a week and a half after leaving Rockall, I was back at my desk at work and leading a normal life!

Having now had the time to reflect on my experience, I realise that I enjoyed the solitude, but was never lonely; there were usually guillemots, gannets and other sea birds to chat to. I watched the minke whales and seals for hours on end, saw sunsets that no-one else on earth experienced, and was visited by racing pigeons, a starling, and the British Antarctic Survey's ship 'James Clark Ross' which came close enough to Rockall for me to shout to the crew. I was even awoken on the morning that I broke the second occupation record by a barrage of fireworks off the stern of the Woods Hole Oceanographic Institution's vessel 'Knorr'. All of these were unique memories that I will keep with me forever.

There were further interviews for TV and radio, which I fitted in around work and family life. One in particular required me to speak at length about the storm. As I went over the memories of that night my heart rate increased, my palms sweated and I felt shaky and nauseous. I don't know if this was some form of post-traumatic stress manifesting, but as time has progressed and with each time I've relayed the story, these symptoms have now all but disappeared.

Quite soon after getting home I had a hankering to return to the rock! For a while I thought it might be as soon as the summer of 2015, but with a proposed Rockall project I was asked to be involved with being postponed for year it may be at least 2016 before I can get back to what has become for me a very special place. I do know that I will return, and I may yet break another record: that of the most landings on Rockall by one individual.

Since returning I have involved Skye Films in postproduction of the footage I shot before and during the expedition, and hope that a short film may result. I was also privileged to have been asked to speak at a TEDx event in Hull.

The Hunterian Museum entomology department analysed the invertebrate samples I collected on the rock and determined that four of the species were new records for Rockall (Appendix A).

Using the two GNSS surveys I ran during the expedition, Ordnance Survey processed the data and calculated, referencing fixed land based stations, that the summit of Rockall is 17.15 metres above global mean sea level (Appendix B), which is approximately one metre lower than had been previously estimated.

In total, the expedition raised over £10,000 for Help for Heroes, and in March 2015, I won English Adventurer of the Year at the National Adventurer Awards in Glasgow for Rockall Solo.

As half expected, after talks I have given on the expedition, and often during interviews, the inevitable question of "What next?" has arisen. I have ideas, but neither my wife nor my work would be happy if I disappeared off again too quickly. All I can say is that this expedition took me five years to organise, and I've had enough of sitting in one spot for so long…

Nick Hancock

Ratho, 2015

APPENDIX A

This article appeared originally in the *Entomologist's Monthly Magazine* and is reproduced by kind permission of Pemberley Books (Publishing).

Entomologist's Monthly Magazine 151: 63–66

Four new invertebrate species including the first insect records from Rockall, Northeast Atlantic Ocean, 2014

BY E. GEOFFREY HANCOCK & NICK HANCOCK

EGH: *The Hunterian (Zoology Museum), University of Glasgow G12 8QQ, Scotland,*
UK email: geoff.hancock@glasgow.ac.uk

Accepted: *October* 22*nd*, 2014

ABSTRACT

The intertidal and terrestrial invertebrates recorded from Rockall islet are discussed together with new records made between 4 June and 23 July 2014 during an author's successful attempt to reside on the rock for more than 45 days.

Keywords: Intertidal and terrestrial invertebrates, new records, Rockall, United Kingdom

INTRODUCTION

The history of observations of invertebrates on Rockall is brief. This note is restricted to intertidal or terrestrial arthropod species. Records of other groups such as molluscs, nematodes, rotifers, oligochaete worms and crustaceans known from earlier visits are not repeated here. Nothing was known before 1955 in which year two mites were found (crisp, 1956). Also prior to the expedition of 2014, the results of which are given here, Professor P.G. Moore landed on top of the rock in 1973. He was unable to descend low enough to satisfy his interests as a professional marine biologist but a few hours were spent sampling and observing diligently and productively and he was able to add another mite to the fauna of the rock (Moore, 1977).

Rockall is an isolated, uninhabited granite islet (total area 784.3m², maximum width 25m) in the northeastern Atlantic Ocean, situated 190 miles west of the St Kilda archipelago and so nearly 240 miles west of the Outer Hebrides of Scotland, at 57°35′77.91″N, 13°41′23.71″W. The second author had the opportunity to collect samples between 4 June and 23 July 2014 during his successful attempt to reside on the rock for more than 45 days (Hancock, 2014). This was both to set a new record for surviving there for that period and to raise money for charitable purposes. The advantage of this situation for recording was that any transient visiting species would have a greater chance of being observed. This is probably the reason for the new records of insects, two Diptera, which may be dispersing at such distances each year but the chances of detection over the sea are extremely small. The wider context of all the new records is discussed below.

TERRESTRIAL ARTHROPOD SPECIES LIST

Previous records of arthropods from Rockall given by Crisp (in Fisher, 1956) and by Moore (1977) are included but this list does not repeat a crustacean and a few non-arthropods collected on those earlier visits. The newly collected specimens from Rockall have been allocated the Hunterian Museum entry number 1428.

ACARI
BDELLIDAE (THE SNOUT MITES)

Bdellodes longirostris (Hermann, 1804)

New record for Rockall; two specimens that correspond to the figures in King (1914) as *Bdella longicornis* (Linn.) and Hull (1915) in respect of key characters given for the palps. Collected amongst algae between Hall's Ledge and summit, 24 June 2014.

HALACARIDAE

Rhombognathopsis armatus (Lohmann, 1893)

This species was found on 21 June 1973 as 15 immature mites in the green algal zone (species of *Prasiola, Blidingia, Bangia*) by Moore (1977) who said that ideally the identity should be confirmed by adult examples.

HYADESIIDAE

Hyadesia fusca (Lohmann, 1894)

A common mite of European rocky shores, several adults found 'among algae high up on the rock' 17 September, 1955 (Crisp, 1956). It was also recorded on 21 June 1973 by Moore (1977) as 'occurring generally' in all the green zone algae.

ORIBATIDAE

Ameronothrus lineatus (Thorell, 1871)

A mite of European rocky shores, one nymph of the genus was found 'among algae high up on the rock' 17 September, 1955 (Crisp, 1956). Moore (1977) collected further examples which included adults that could be identified as *A. lineatus* (Thorell, 1871) from a crevice above the pool on Hall's Ledge which is also above the main *Prasiola* zone.

IXODIDAE

Ixodes uriae White, 1852

New record for Rockall; nymphs (second instar). Collected within the survival pod on collector's leg, 6 July and another on the arm, 12 July 2014, presumably attracted by human body warmth in the absence of the normal host. This species is the common sea bird tick that leaves its host to moult between feeds.

INSECTA – DIPTERA
SYRPHIDAE

Episyrphus balteatus (De Geer, 1776)

New record for Rockall, one female. A strongly migratory hoverfly also known from Faroes (Jensen, 2001) and Iceland. Caught on the outside of the survival pod, 10 June 2014.

DROSOPHILDAE

Scaptomyza pallida (Zetterstedt, 1847)

New record for Rockall, two males and one female. According to Bächli *et. al.* (2004) this is very widespread and has been found as far north as Torsvag, Norway and previously recorded from the Faroes and Iceland. Caught on the outside of the survival pod, 10 June 2014.

DISCUSSION

There are a number of interesting aspects to these records. All four of the 2014 species records are new to Rockall but none of the species previously seen were amongst the samples. The lack of insect records on earlier visits is not surprising as their presence is fortuitous and someone staying on Rockall for only a few hours has less chance to encounter them. The complete lack of flowering plants means there is no provision for any such insect to maintain a population.

The fruit fly *Scaptomyza pallida* is found worldwide which may be due to distribution through human movements and trade. Paul Beuk (pers. com., email, 15 August 2014) has recorded it as a common element of the aerial plankton up to an altitude of at least 3km. It was the only species of drosophilid found in these aerial samples that he has examined. Thus it has a potential to colonise some other regions naturally, although only in the direction of air currents and prevailing winds. It is conjectured that these flies appeared on Rockall due to some weather conditions that created appropriate air currents. although the hoverfly *Episyrphus balteatus* exhibits a directed migratory pattern, as both the fly species were caught on the same day some aspect of the wind current and direction may be responsible for their joint appearance; their capture a product of the same conditions. The yellow colour of the pod on which the insects settled would have attracted the flies once within sight of it.

The sea bird tick may not be present in all seasons and is more likely to be encountered during periods when birds are roosting or attempting to nest. There are no confirmed records of sea birds succeeding in rearing chicks on Rockall but several reliable observations of attempts being made (Fisher, 1956). These would allow time for a sea bird tick to feed and leave one host between instars in anticipation of locating a new one and continue development.

The bdellid is predatory, as are the other mite species and may be feeding on the other mites or small invertebrates co-inhabiting the rock crevices. The three mites found by Moore (1977) and to which now can be added the *Bdella* species, were described by him as 'regular inhabitants of the littoral zone ... [and] represent a high shore recurrent group characteristic of wave exposed places'. The other invertebrates known from Rockall are tardigrades, nematodes and oligochaete worms which could form part of their diet (Pugh & King, 1985; Moore, 1977). King (1914) recorded *Bdella longirostris* (as *longicornis* (Linn.)) in the Clyde estuary and Hull (1915) provides a key to species. The transient nature of populations of such animals affected by the extreme wave and wind conditions on Rockall may explain changes in species composition over time.

ACKNOWLEDGEMENTS

Geoff Moore kindly donated the mites from his 1973 visit to Rockall to the Hunterian Museum (entry number 1429) following an enquiry. Christina M. Berry, Institute of Biodiversity, Animal Health and Comparative Medicine, University of Glasgow, confirmed the identity of the ixodine tick and Paul Beuk, Natuurhistorisch Museum Maastricht, is thanked for his prompt response to our query on the drosophilid.

REFERENCES

Bächli, G., Vilela, C.R., Escher, S.A. & Saura, A., 2004, The Drosophilidae (Diptera) of Fennoscandia, *Fauna Entomologica Scandinavica*, **39**: 1–362.

Crisp, D.J., 1956, The intertidal zoology of Rockall, pp. 177–179 (Appendix 3). *In*: Fisher, J., 1956, *Rockall*, London.

Fisher, J., 1956, *Rockall*, London.

Hancock, N., 2014, website http://www.rockallsolo.com [accessed September 2014].

Hull, J.E., 1915, The snout mites, *The Vasculum*, **1**: 117–123.

Jensen, J.-K., 2001, Faroese Hoverflies (Diptera: Syrphidae): checklist to the year 2000, *Fróðskaparrit*, **48**: 125–133.

King, L.A.L., 1914, Notes on the habits and characteristics of some littoral mites of Millport, *Proceedings of the Royal Physical Society of Edinburgh*, **29**: 129–141.

Moore, P.G., 1977, Additions to the littoral fauna of Rockall, with a description of *Araeolamus penelope* sp. nov. (Nematoda: Axonolaimidae), *Journal of the Marine Biological Association of the United Kingdom*, **57**: 191–200.

Pugh, P.J.A. & King, P.E., 1985, Feeding in intertidal Acari, *Journal of Experimental Marine Biology and Ecology*, **94**: 269–280.

APPENDIX B

ORDNANCE SURVEY REPORT

From: Mark Greaves
To: Nick Hancock
Date: 17/09/2014

Hi Nick,

Final coordinates of Rockall are:
ETRS89 XYZ: 3328852.7978, -810705.6545, 5361843.3423;
ETRS89 lat, long, H: N 57 35 46.694702, W 13 41 14.308269, 77.680;

The height H above is relative to the ellipsoid so an approximation to a height above mean sea level needs to be determined using a geoid model. The OS geoid model OSGM02 does not cover Rockall but there are several online tools available. Using the tool here:

```
http://www.unavco.org/software/geodetic-utilities/geoid-
height-calculator/geoid-height-calculator.html
```

gives a mean sea level height of approx. 17.22m. Using this tool:

```
http://geographiclib.sourceforge.net/cgi-
bin/GeoidEval?input=57.59630408393+-
13.687307852593&option=Submit
```

gives 17.10m, 17.22m or 17.85m depending on the geoid model used. Ignoring the 17.85 result which is from an old model and taking the results from the 1996 and 2008 models it is clear that the mean sea level height of Rockall is in the region of 17.15m. A bit of background to the processing:

I split your data sets at midnight to give 4 sessions of data – 13 & 14th June and 14 & 15th July. The split at midnight made the data compatible with all the external precise products (e.g. satellite orbits) used in the processing.

I included data from Ordnance Survey stations – ARIS, BARR, BENB, INVR, KINL, LCAR, STOR and TIRE. I also included data from ARGI in the Faroes, FOYL in Northern Ireland and HOFN in Iceland. This gave a good spread of data around Rockall which helped get the best estimation of atmospheric errors especially ones from the Troposphere. A map of OS stations is here:

http://www.ordnancesurvey.co.uk/gps/os-net-rinex-data/

and a map showing the other stations is here:

http://www.epncb.oma.be/_networkdata/stationmaps.php

I used the same processing software and methods as we use to determine new coordinates for our own stations. The results from the 4 sessions of data showed very good precision with a comparison of coordinates from each session agreeing at the sub 5mm level.

A "coordinate recovery" quality check was performed on the final completed data set spanning all 4 sessions. This is where all the computed baselines radiate out from Rockall so that the data collected there has an influence on all the other coordinates. Only a single station's coordinates are fixed and the resulting coordinates of the surrounding stations are compared to their correct values. The resulting differences indicate the quality of the whole solution and especially of the data from Rockall. The coordinate recovery check indicates that the solution gives coordinates accurate to better than 2cm in all directions.

The final coordinates were obtained by constraining the OS stations to their known coordinates.

Best regards

Mark
Ordnance Survey
Adanac Drive
Southampton SO16 0AS
http://www.ordnancesurvey.co.uk

APPENDIX C

BIBLIOGRAPHY

Martin Martin, A Late voyage to St. Kilda, 1698

de Kerguelen Tremarec (1771) Relation d'un voyage dans la mer du nord, ...fait en 1767 et 1768, Paris

Purdy, John (1812) Memoir of a chart of the Atlantic, London

Basil Hall, Fragments of Voyages and Travels, Vol. 3, 1831

Barrow, John, ed. (1852) The geography of Hudson's Bay: being the remarks of Captain W. Coats..., London, Hakluyt Soc.

Miller Christy F.L.S. (1898) Rockall, Scottish Geographical Magazine, 14:8, 393-415

James A. Macintosh, Rockall, Hugh MacDonald Ltd., 1946

Little G.A, Brendan the Navigator, M.H. Gill and Son, 1946

James Fisher, Rockall, The Country Book Club, 1957

Island of Rockall Act 1972

Holland GS & Gardiner RA (1975) The First Map of Rockall, The Geographical Journal; Vol 141; Part 1

Paul Campbell, A Landing on Rockall, The Royal Cruising Club Journal, 1975

British Tertiary Volcanic Provenance, Geological Conservation Review Series, No.4, Chapman and Hall, London, 1992

Martin Lyster, The Strange Adventures of the Dangerous Sports Club, The Do-Not Press, 1997

Chris Rose, The Turning of the 'Spar, Greenpeace, 1998

Ben Fogle, In Search of an Island of My Own, Penguin Books, 2006

MacDonald F (2006) The last outpost of Empire: Rockall and the Cold War, Journal of Historical Geography, Vol. 32, No. 3, 2006, p.627-647

ACKNOWLEDGMENTS

Although this expedition was called 'Rockall Solo', I could not have been successful without the help, advice, input and understanding of many people and companies. My thanks are due, in no particular order, for their assistance and advice, and both direct and indirect support, to:

Pam Hancock, Jamie McKay, Piers Lecheminant, Alex Hancock, Peter Boyd-Cross, Ben and Sarah Reynolds, Sandy McKeand, Mike Boyle, Chris Stewart, Niall Iain MacDonald, Fraser MacDonald, Stevie Young, Damian Sorgiovanni, Angus Campbell, Angus Smith, Pete Macdonald, Alastair Morrison, Ruari Beaton, Pennie Latin, Jane Tubb, Sarah Outen, Bob Kerr, Michael Schofield, Nick Sharpe, Torquil Crichton, John and Harvey, Ben Saunders, Andy Cave, Dan and Ann Parry, Rupert Barker, Al Baker, Tim Raub, Michael Metcalfe, Geoff Hancock, Tom McClean, Leven Brown, Mark Beaumont, Ken Hitchen, Alison Abbott, James Rockall, Paul Blacklock, Graham Hart-Ives, Murray Webster, John and James Muir, Richard Canvin, Colin and Fiona Paten, Andrew Bell, and Norman and Morag Macleod.

Calor, DM Hall LLP, LPG Exceptional Energy, WLPGA, Inmarsat, Wireless Innovation, Kukri, Northgate Vehicle Hire, Webster Power Products, Ergo Computing, Smiths of Dean Drums, Kilda Cruises, Portable Winch, The Bridge Inn, Edinburgh International Climbing Arena (EICA), The Seagull Trust, Dovecote Park, Claymore Security, Lickisto Blackhouse Camping, Am Bothan Bunkhouse, Caledonian MacBrayne, Trailer Engineering, William Hacket Chains, Ampair Energy, Help for Heroes, Just Stainless, The Hunterian Museum, Ordnance Survey, Leica Geosystems, St. Andrew's University, Abhainn Dearg, Charterhouse, Gilberts Architects, Foam Spray Tech, Pyramid Display Products, Lewmar, Icon Films, Safety Lifting Gear, Atlantic Marine Services, Summit Rescue, Greenpeace, Telespazio Vega, Ratho Byres Forge, and Skye Films.